I0510323

COLORING BOOK FOR ADULTS

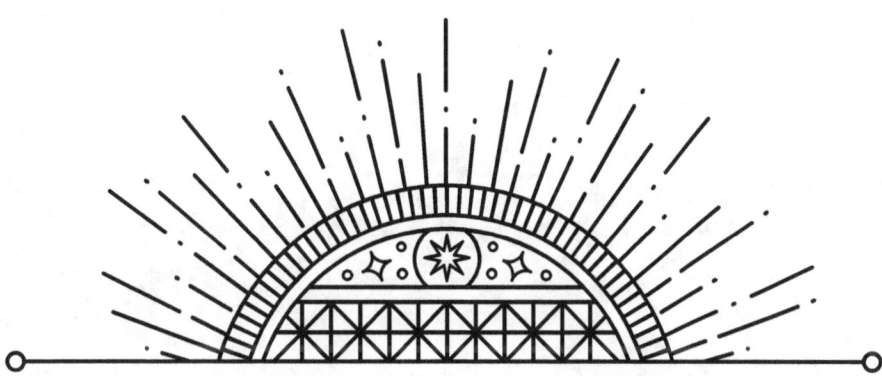

THIS BOOK BELONGS TO:

- - - - - - - - - -

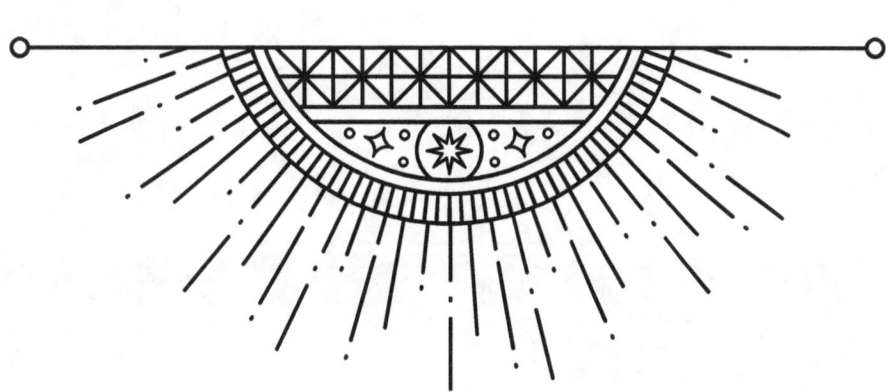

BEACH

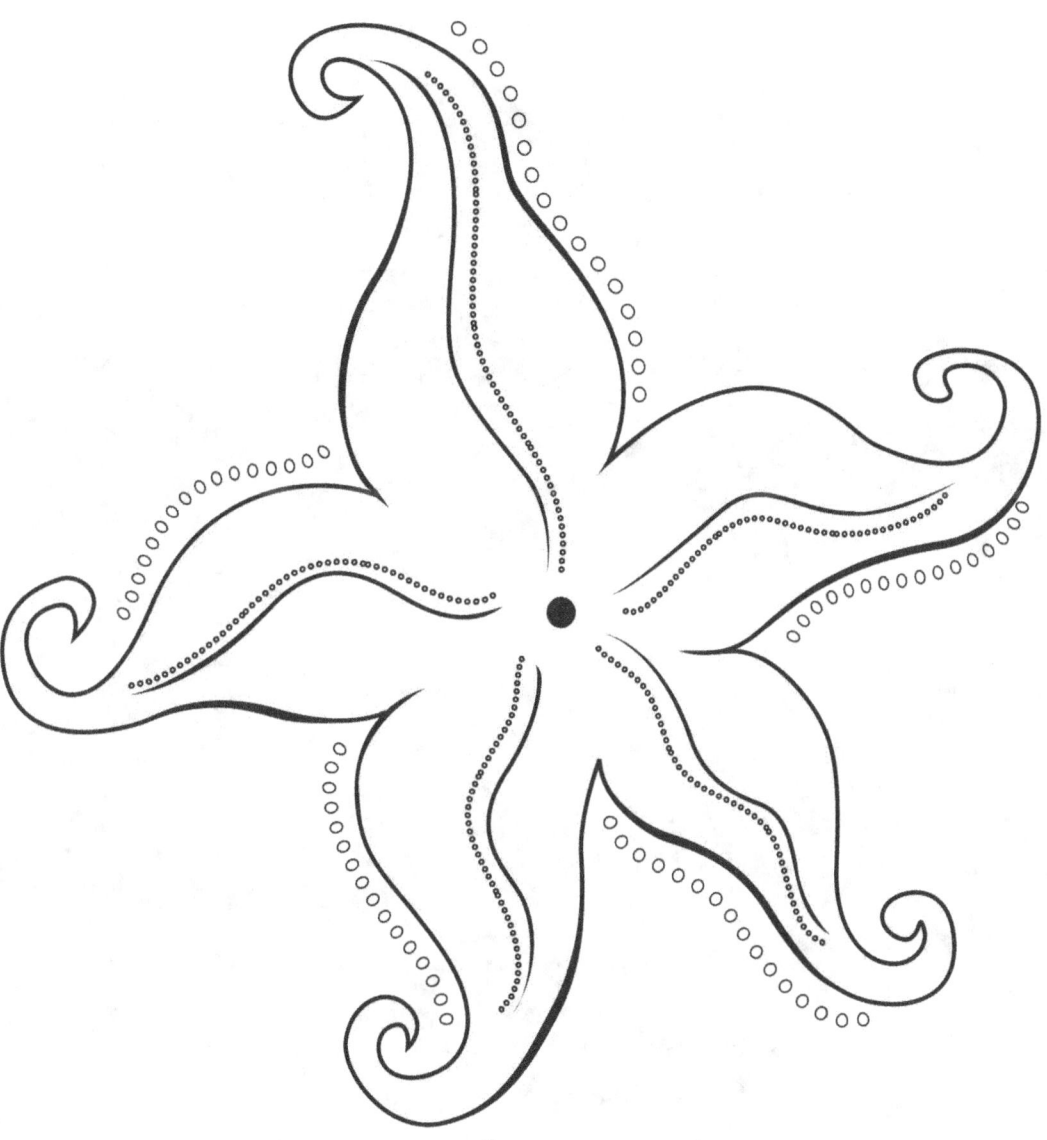

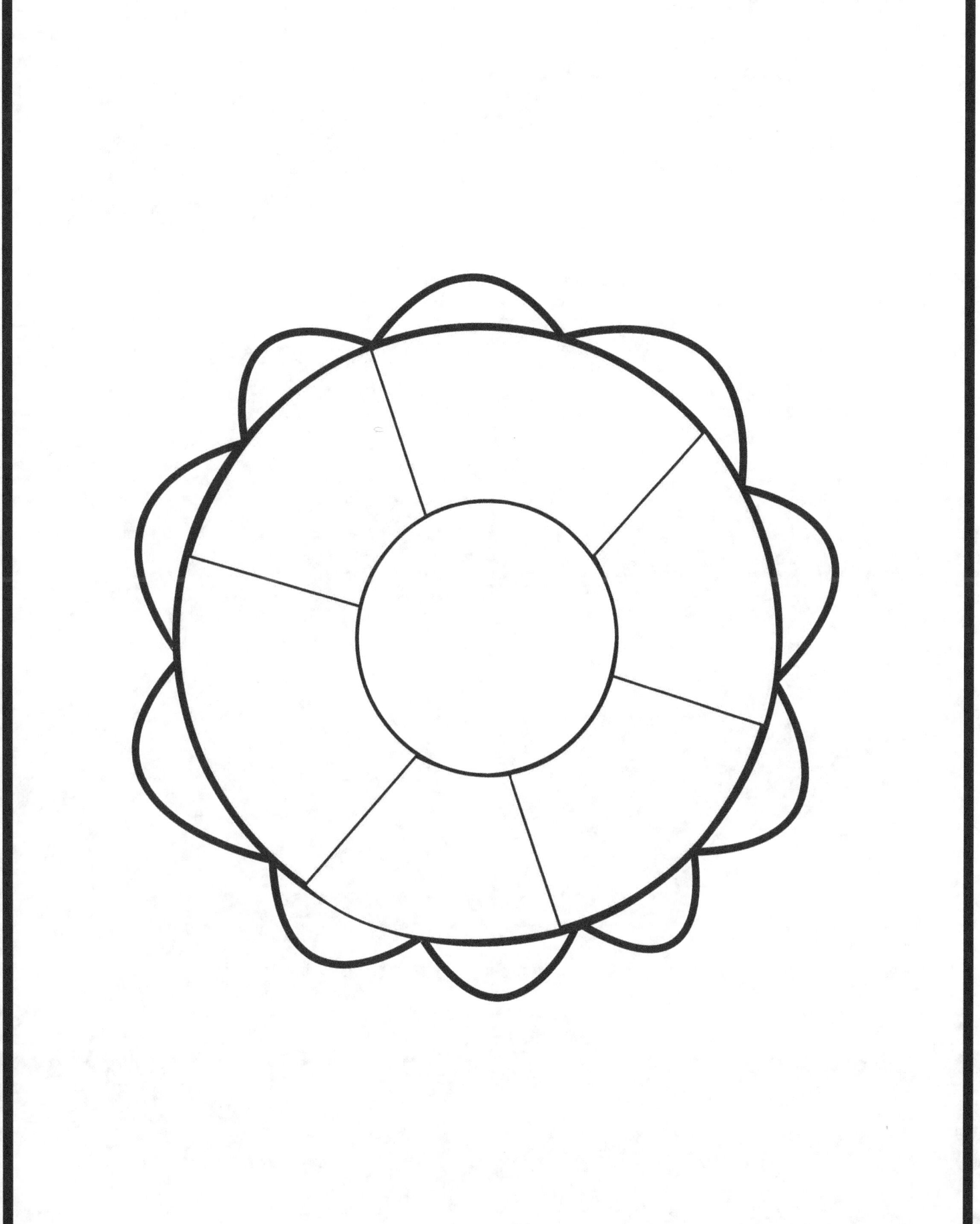

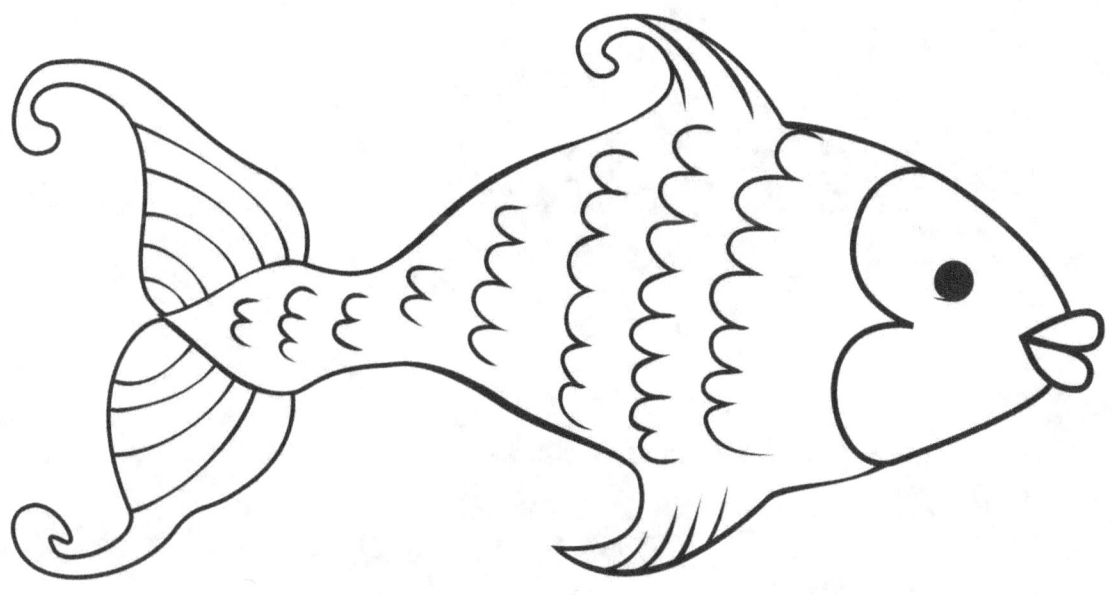

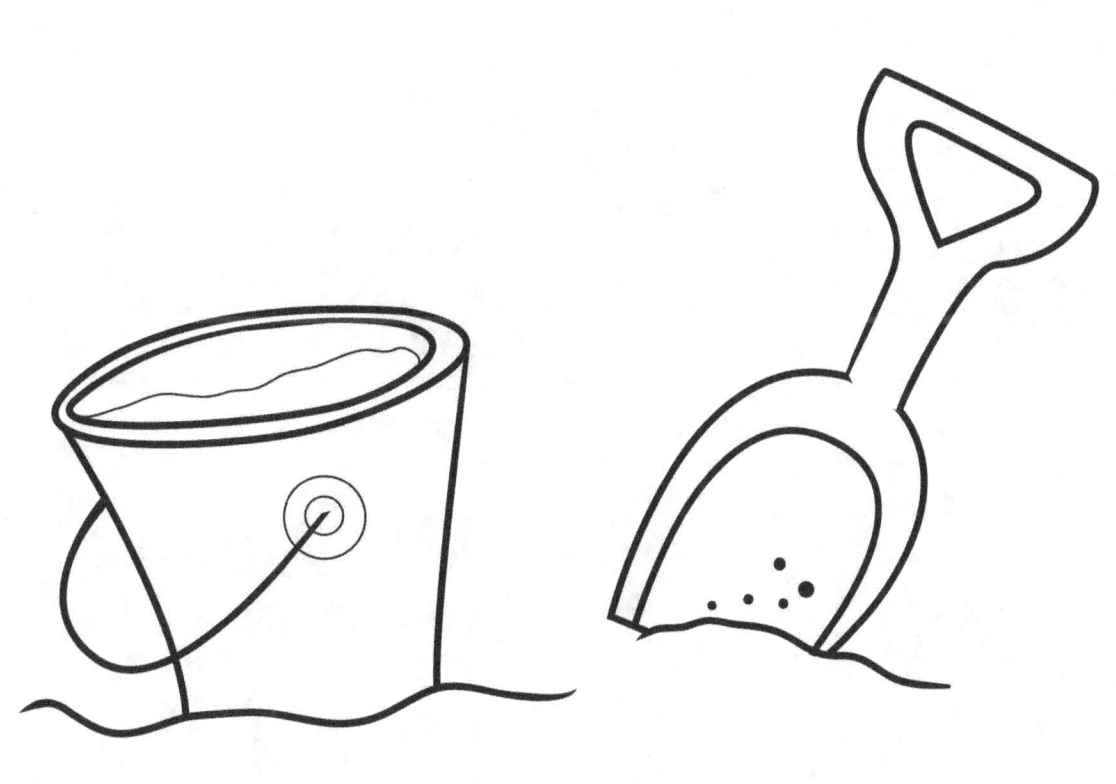

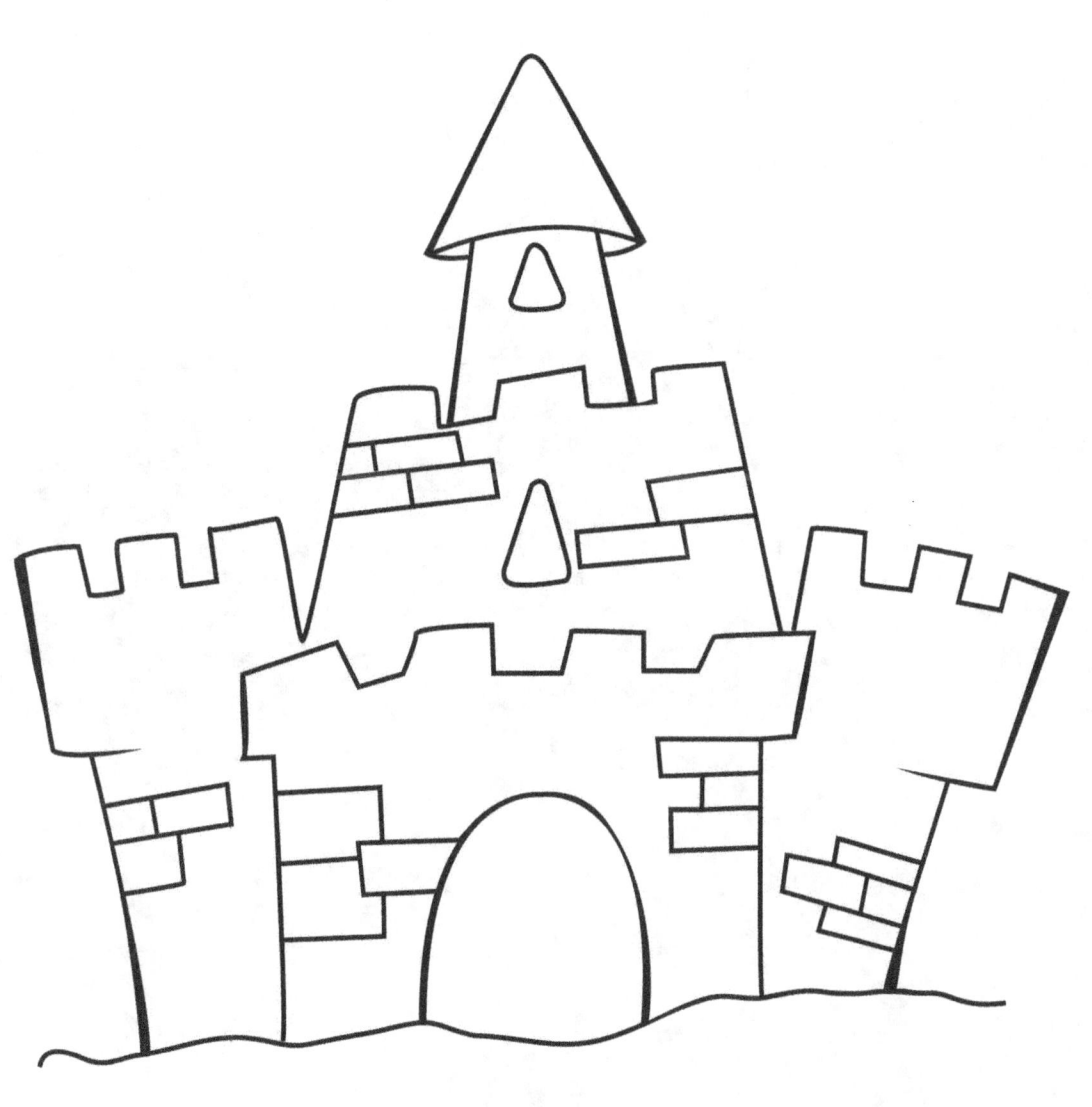

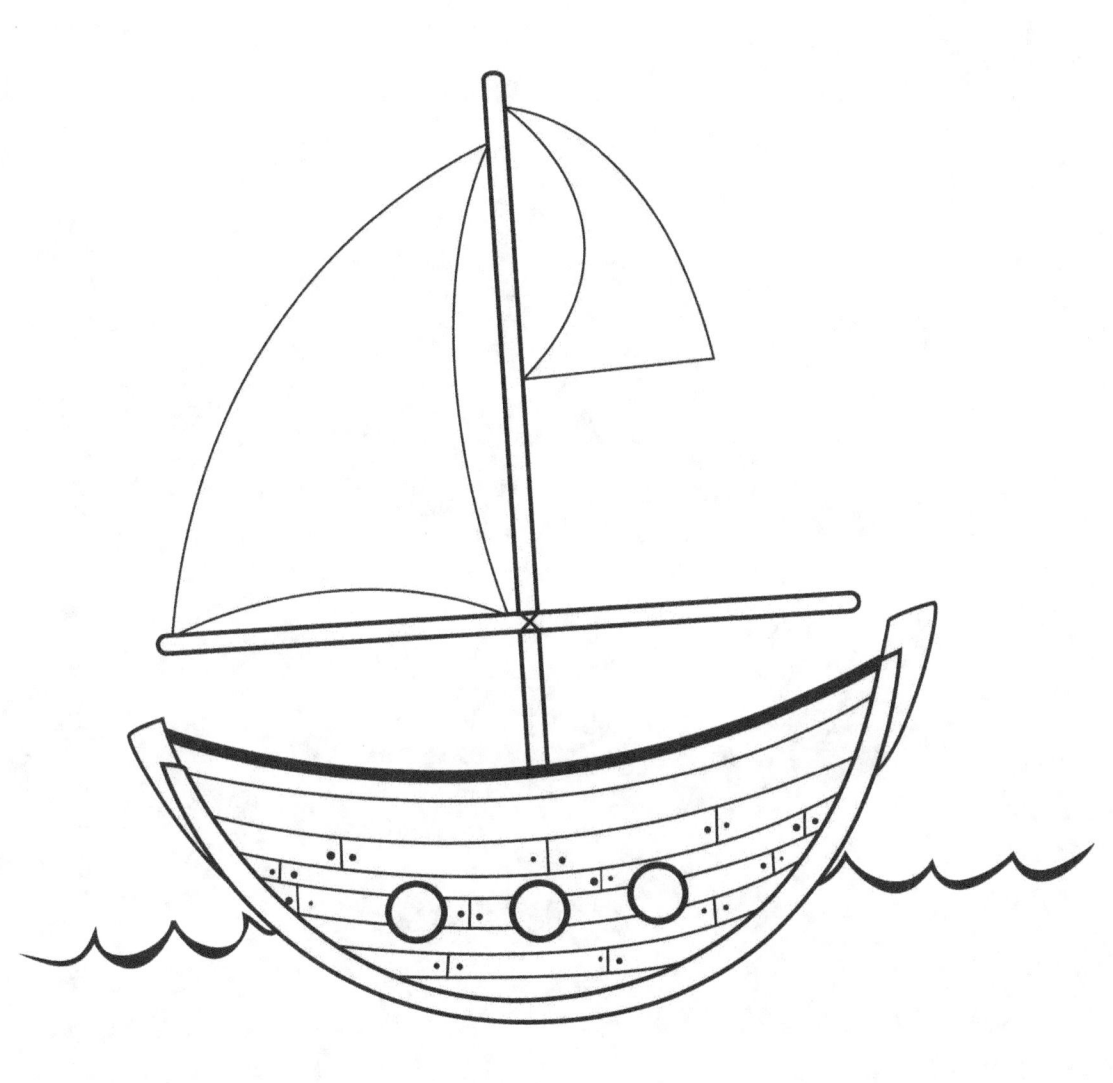

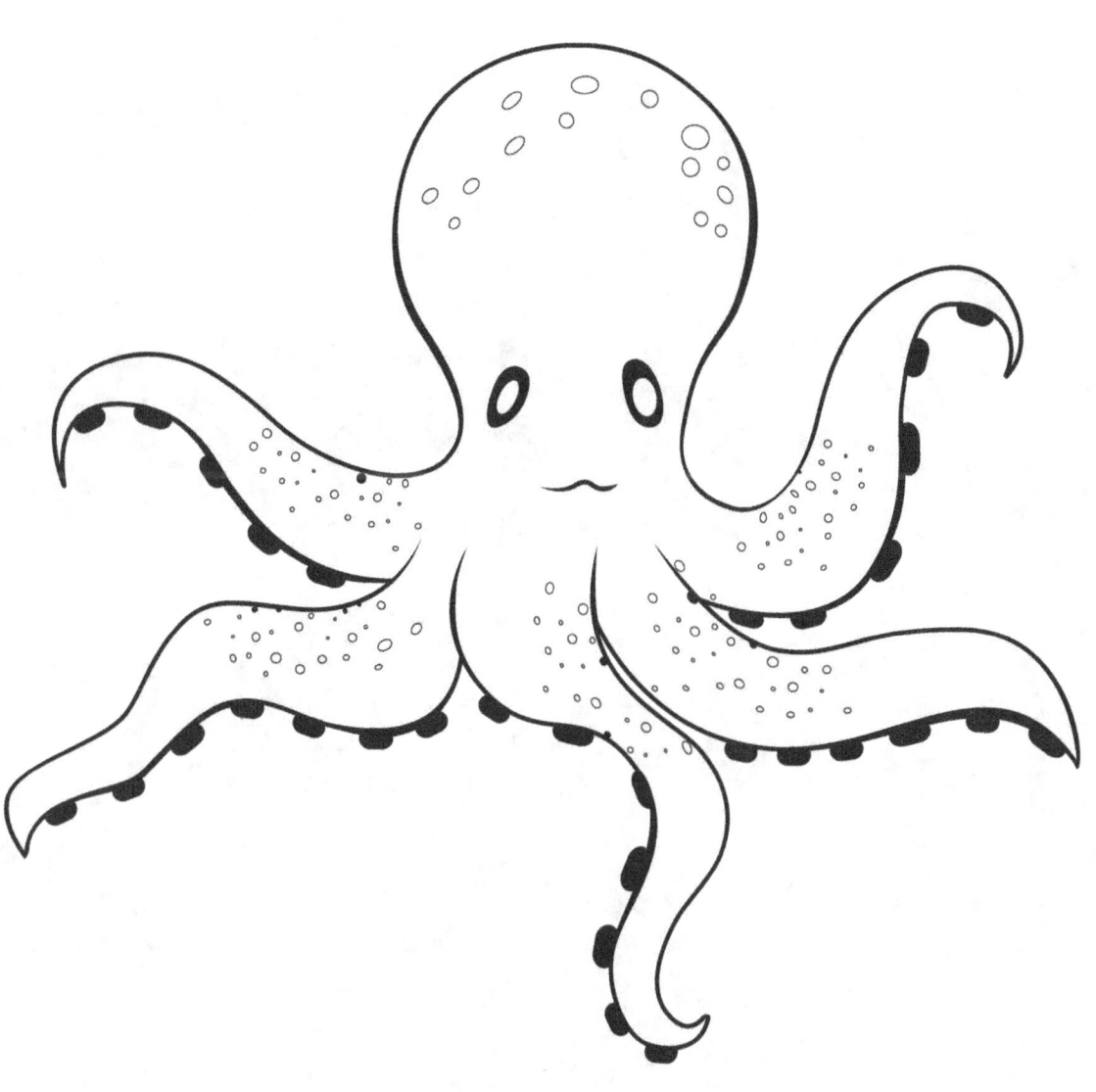

TEA

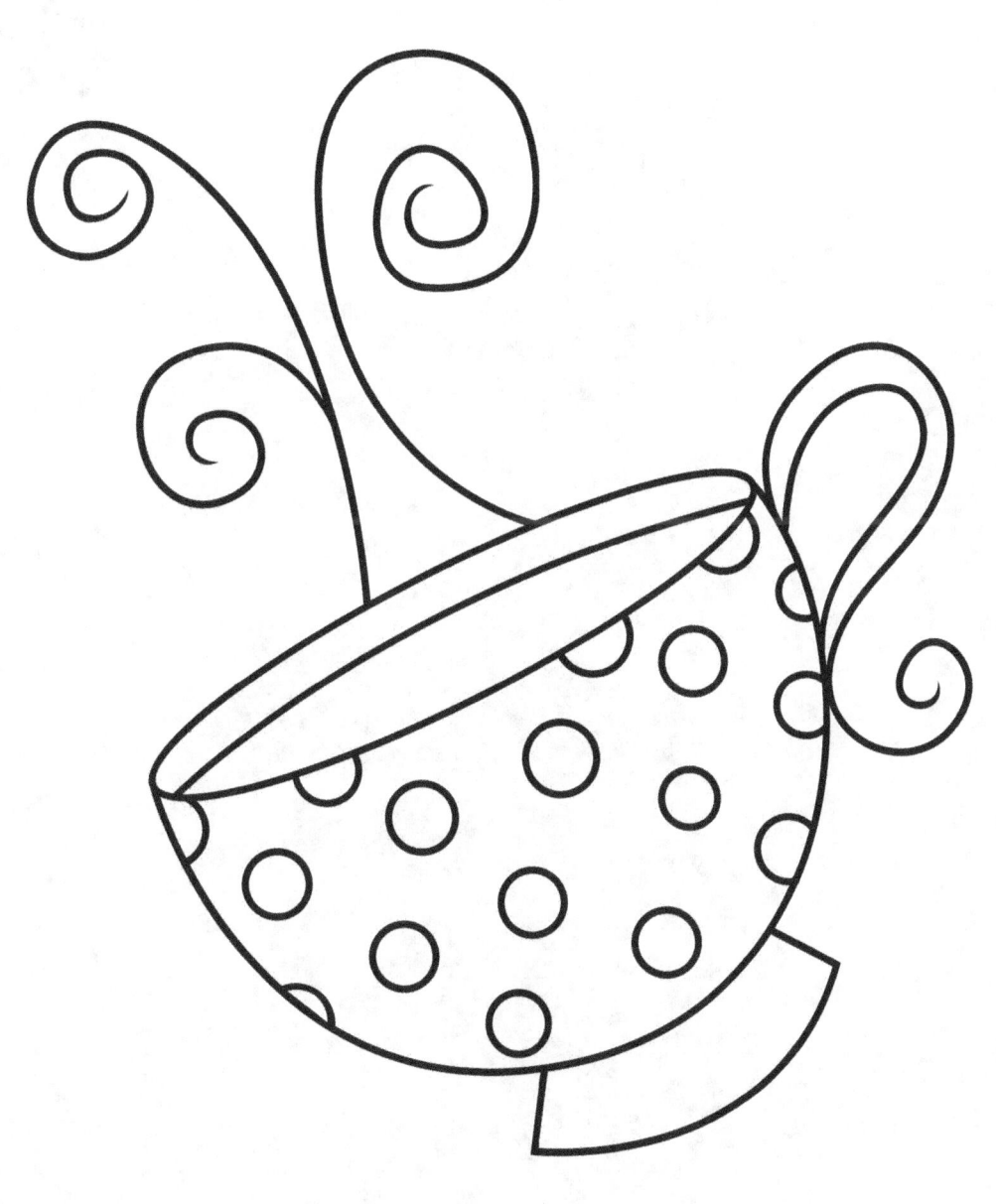

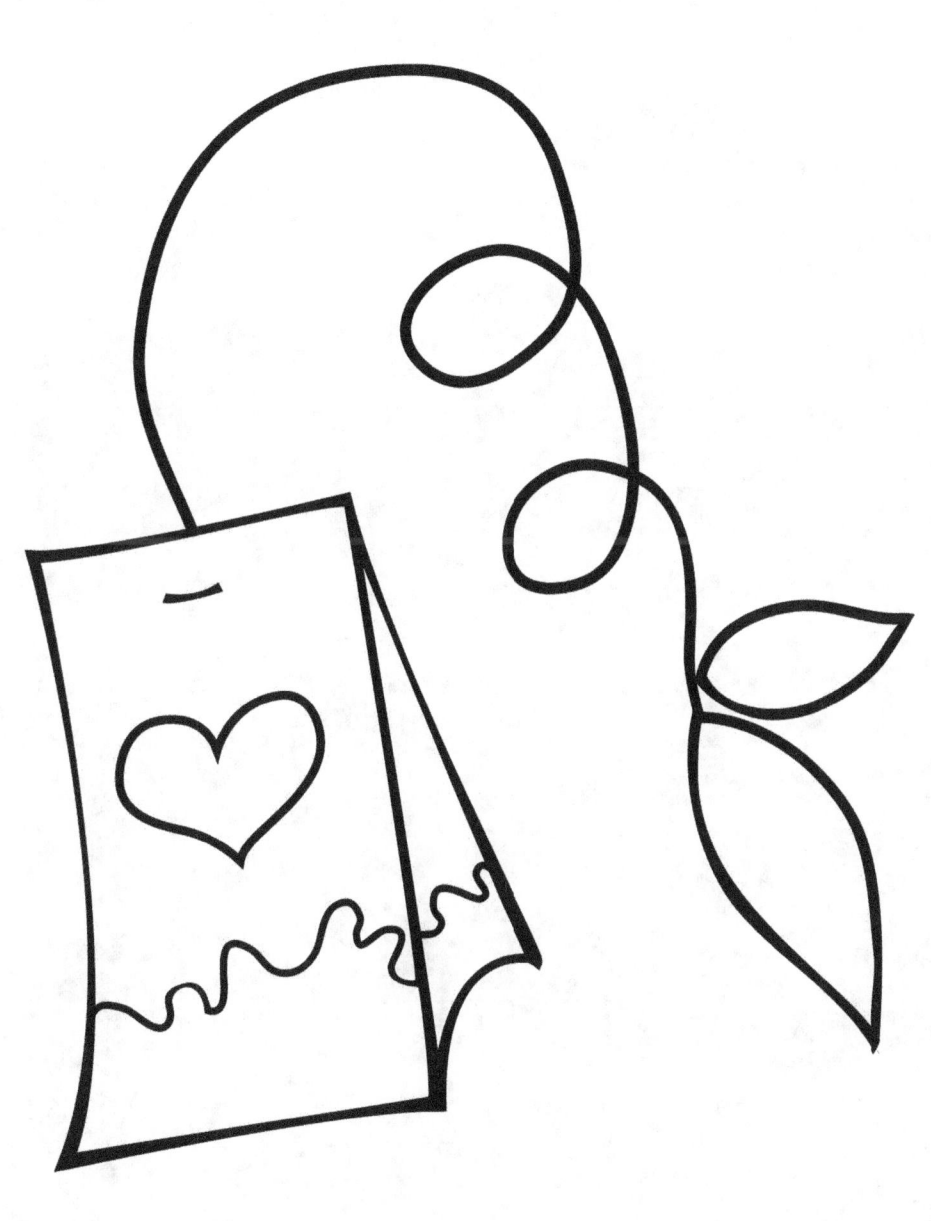

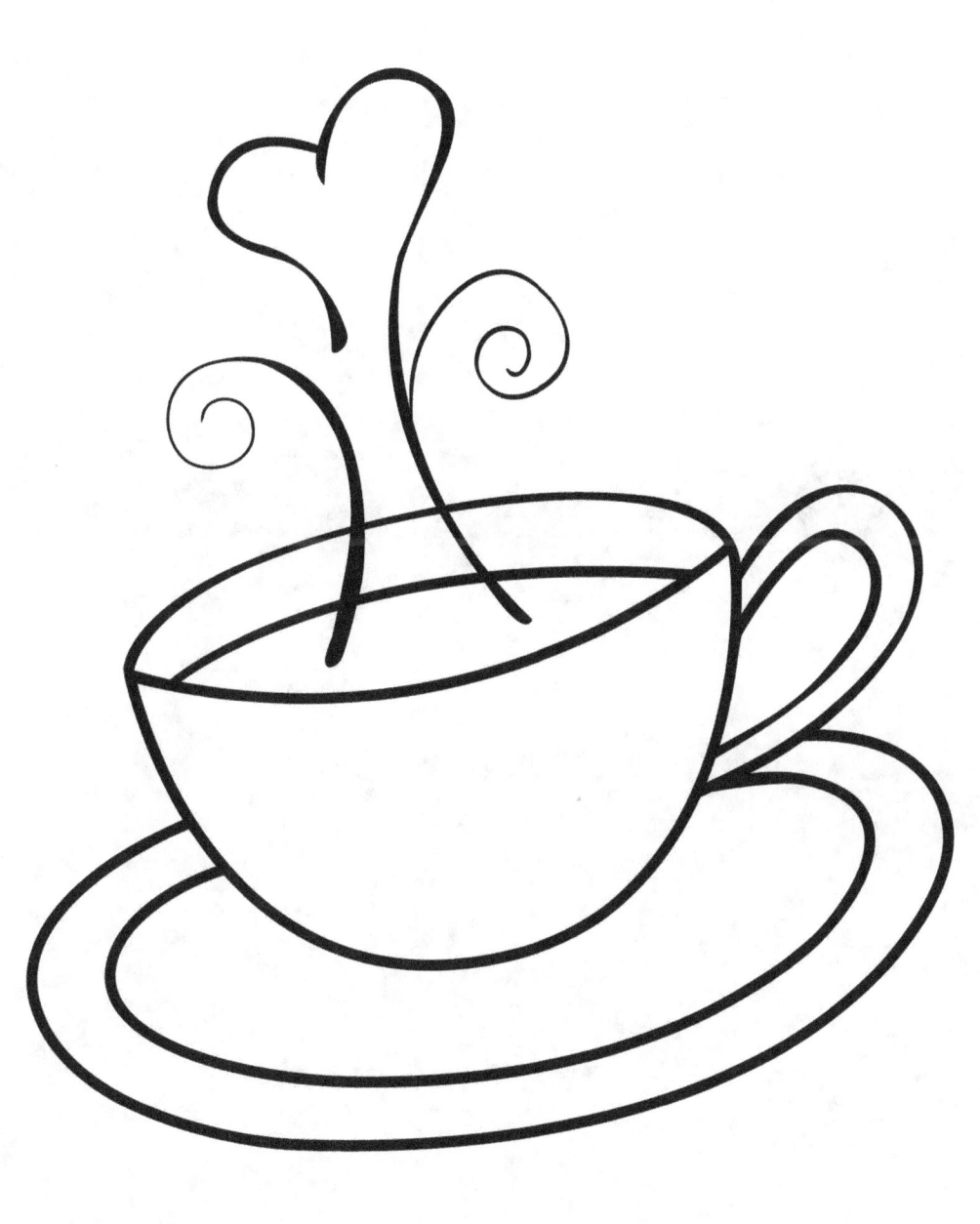

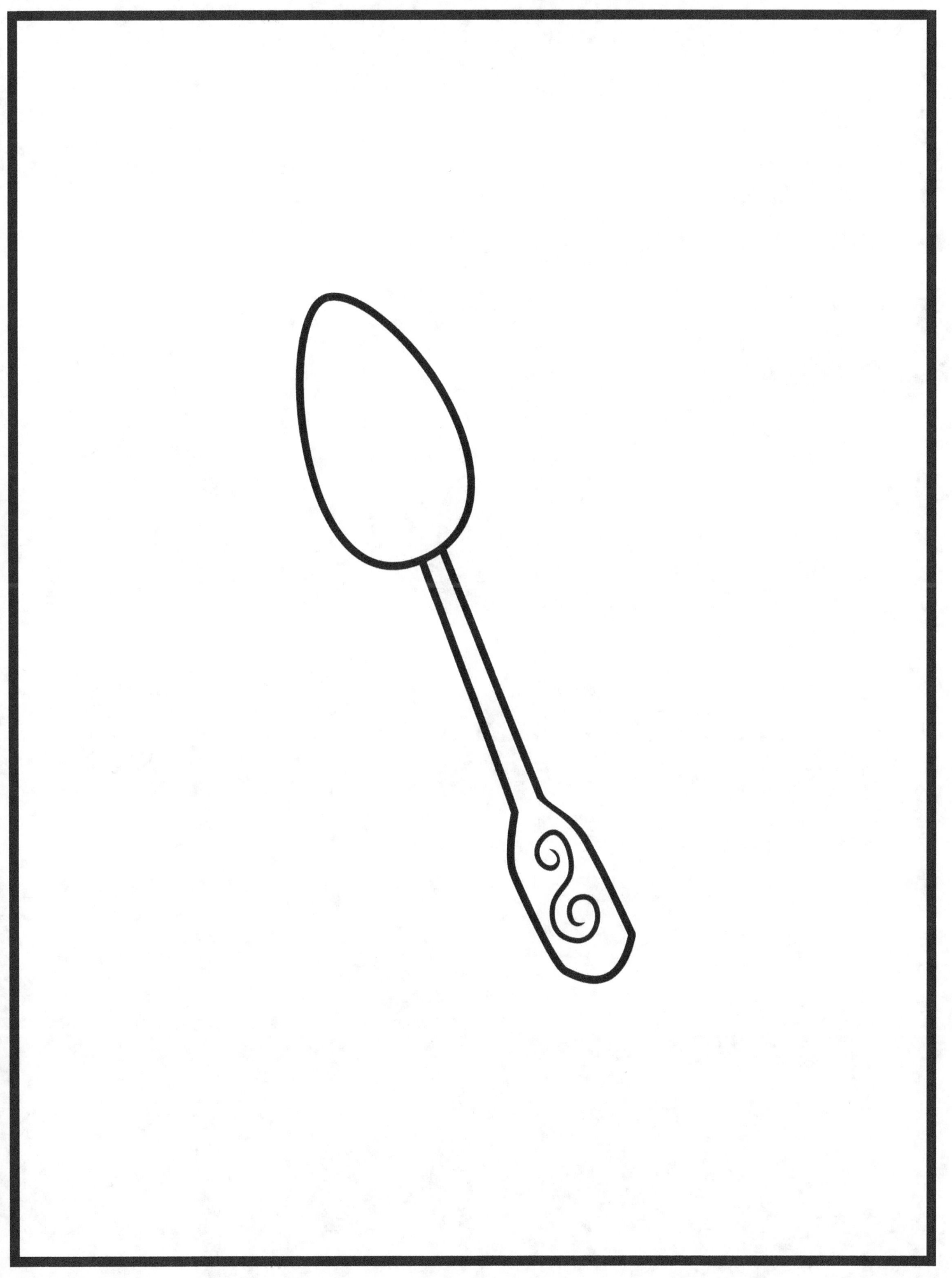

PERFUME

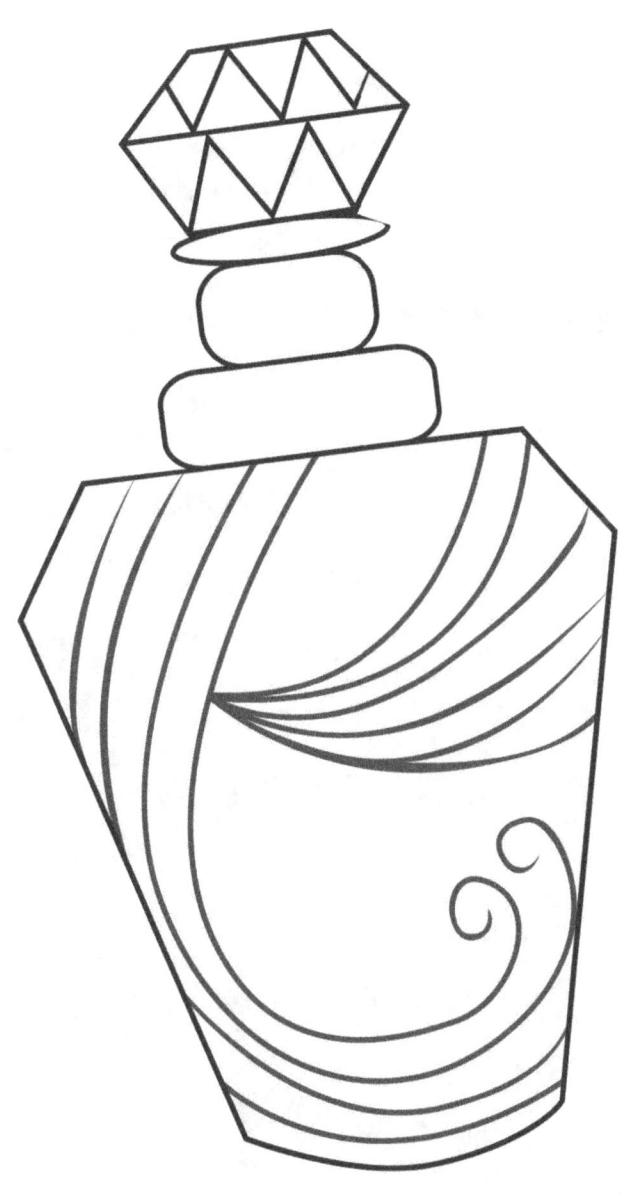

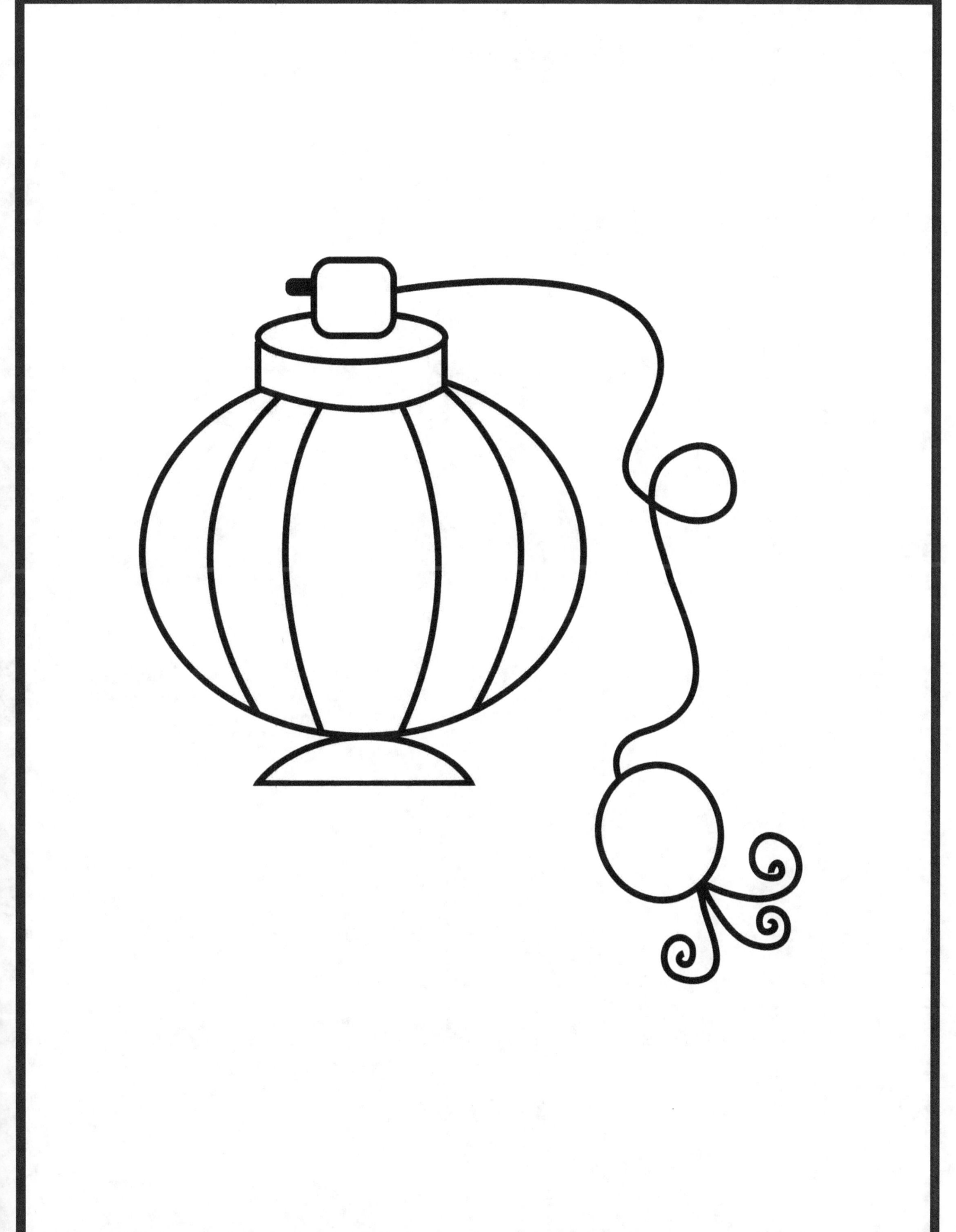

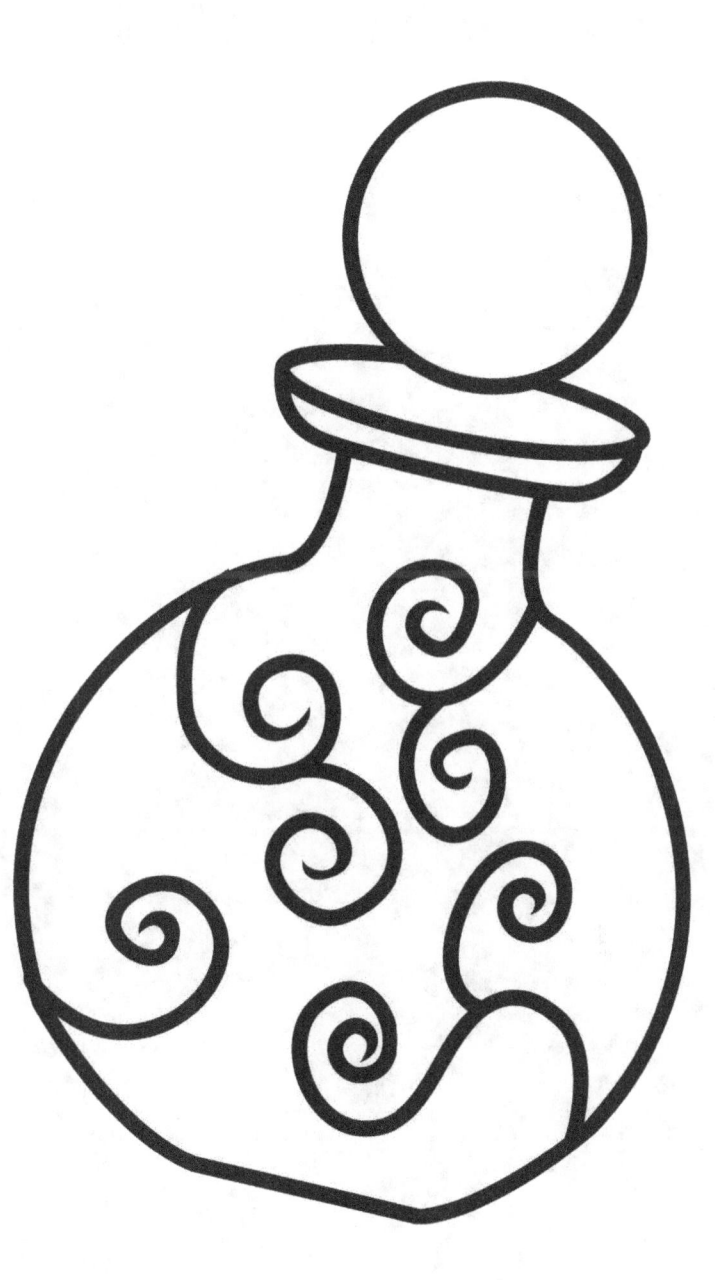

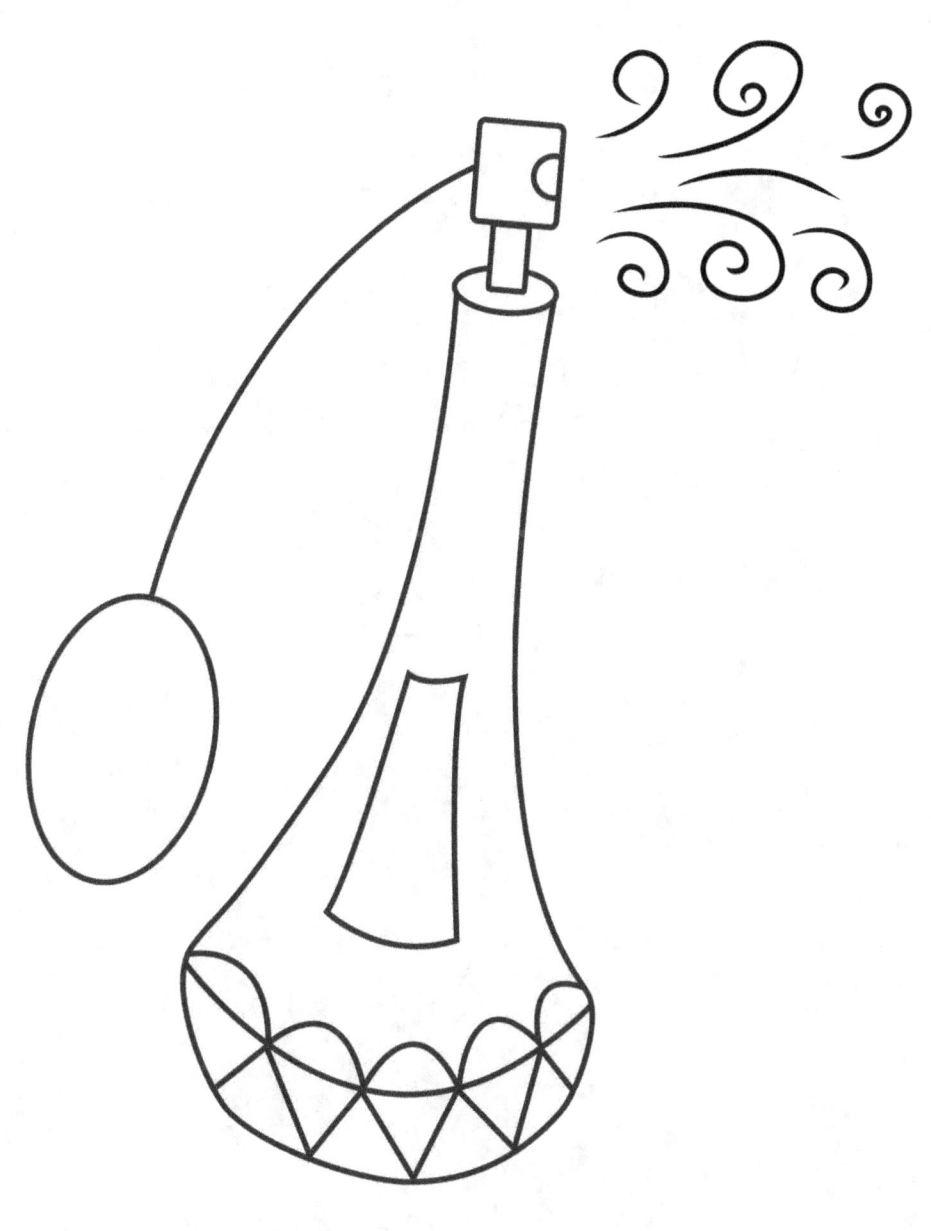

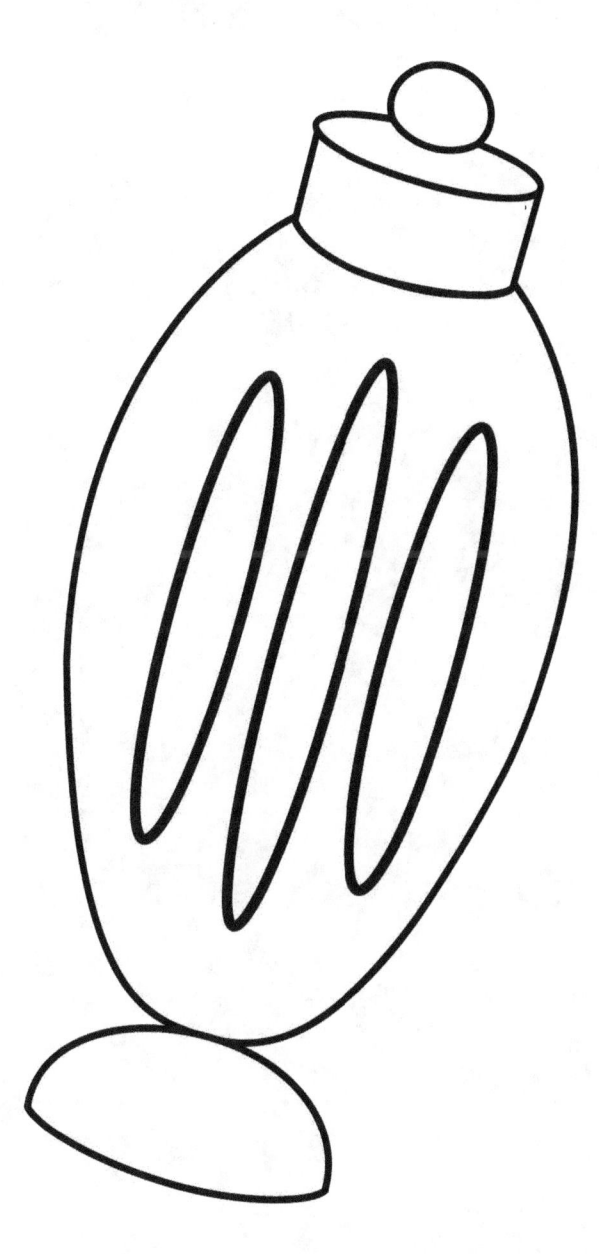

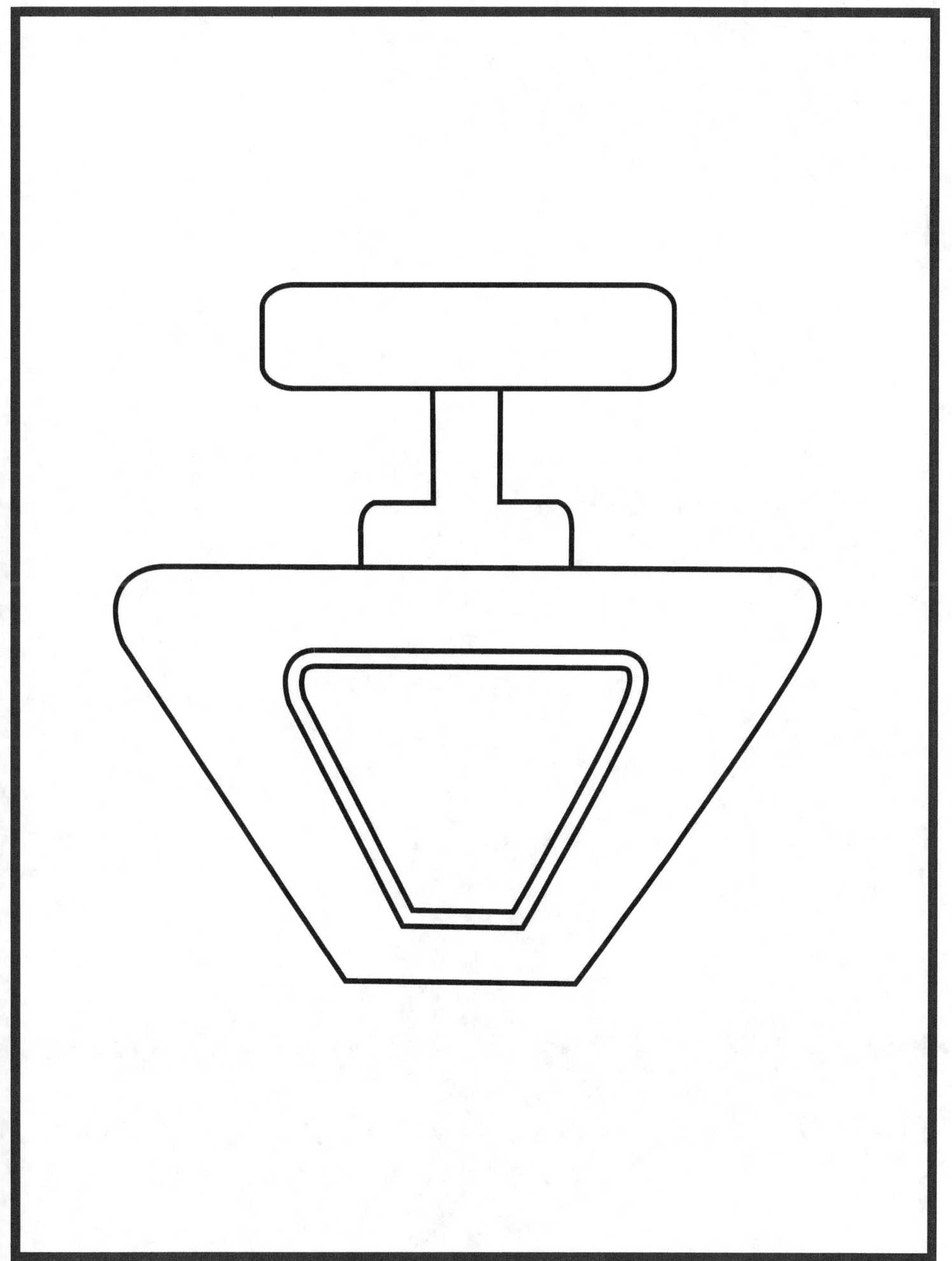

BAKING

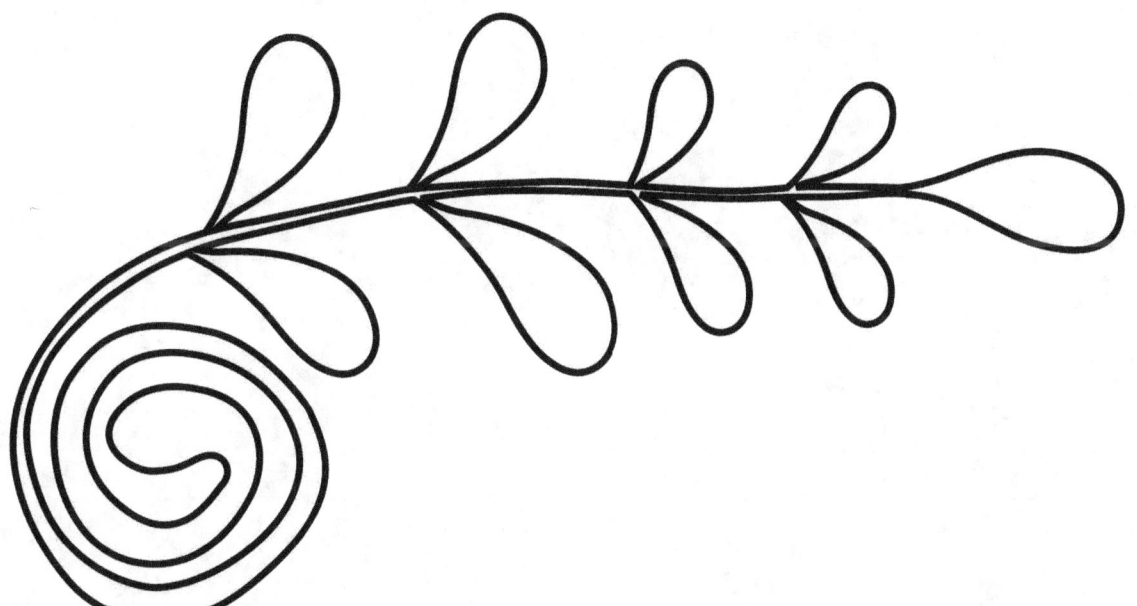

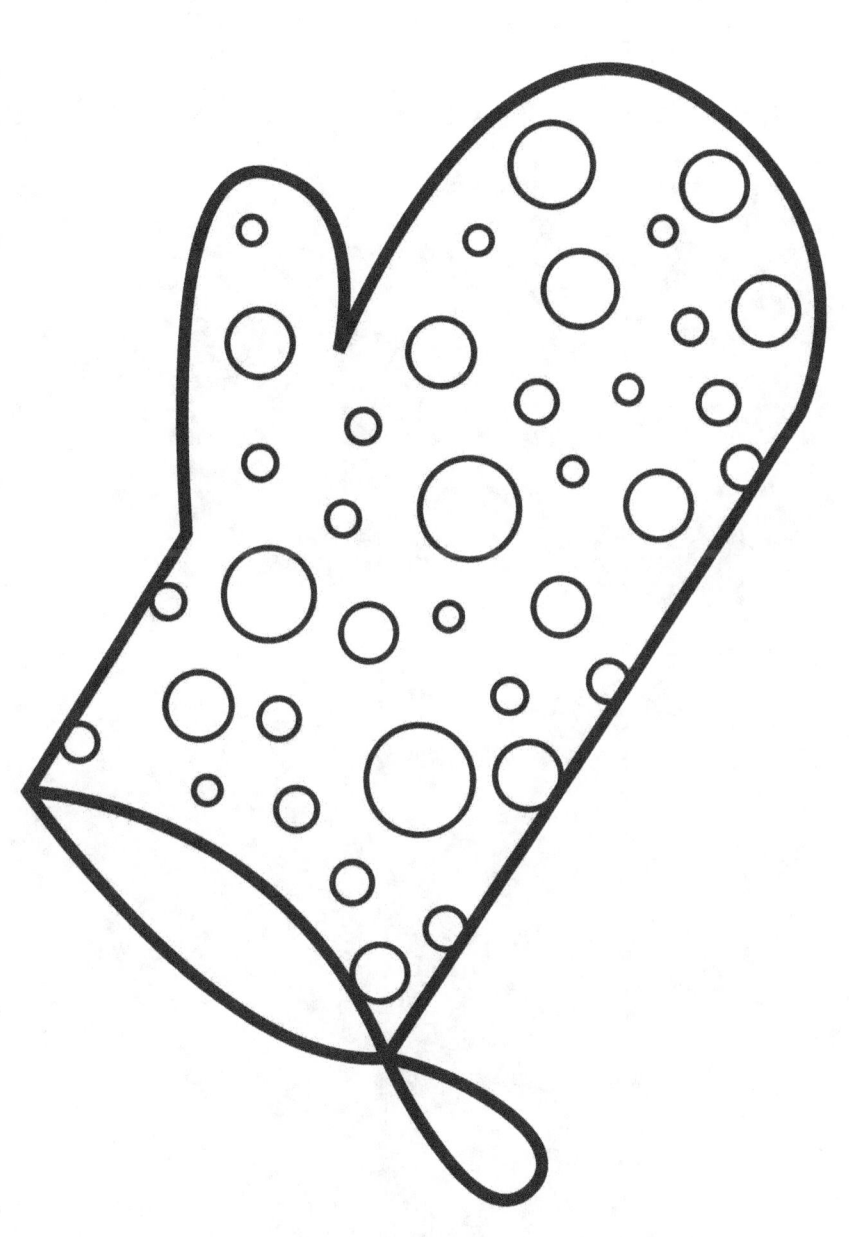

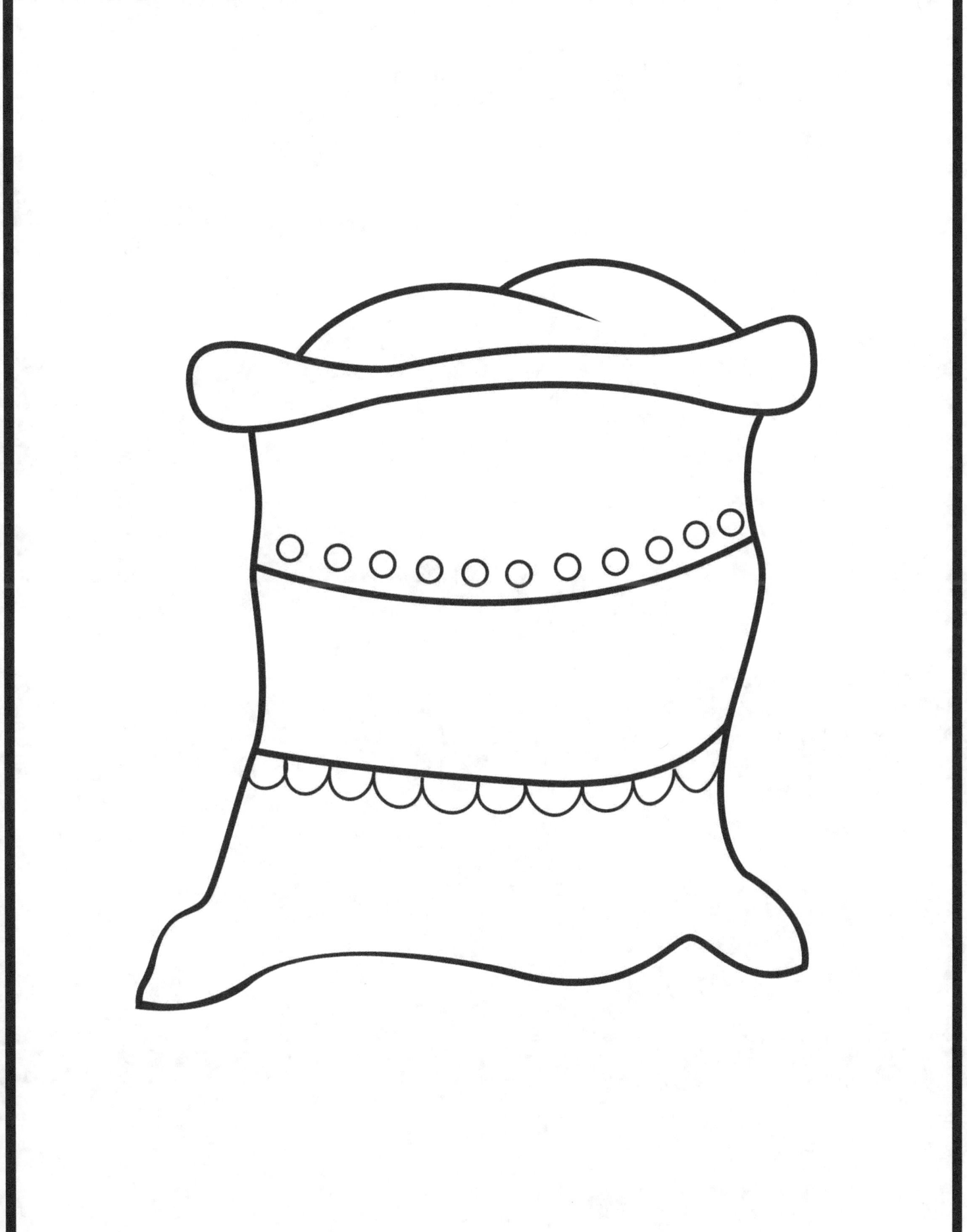

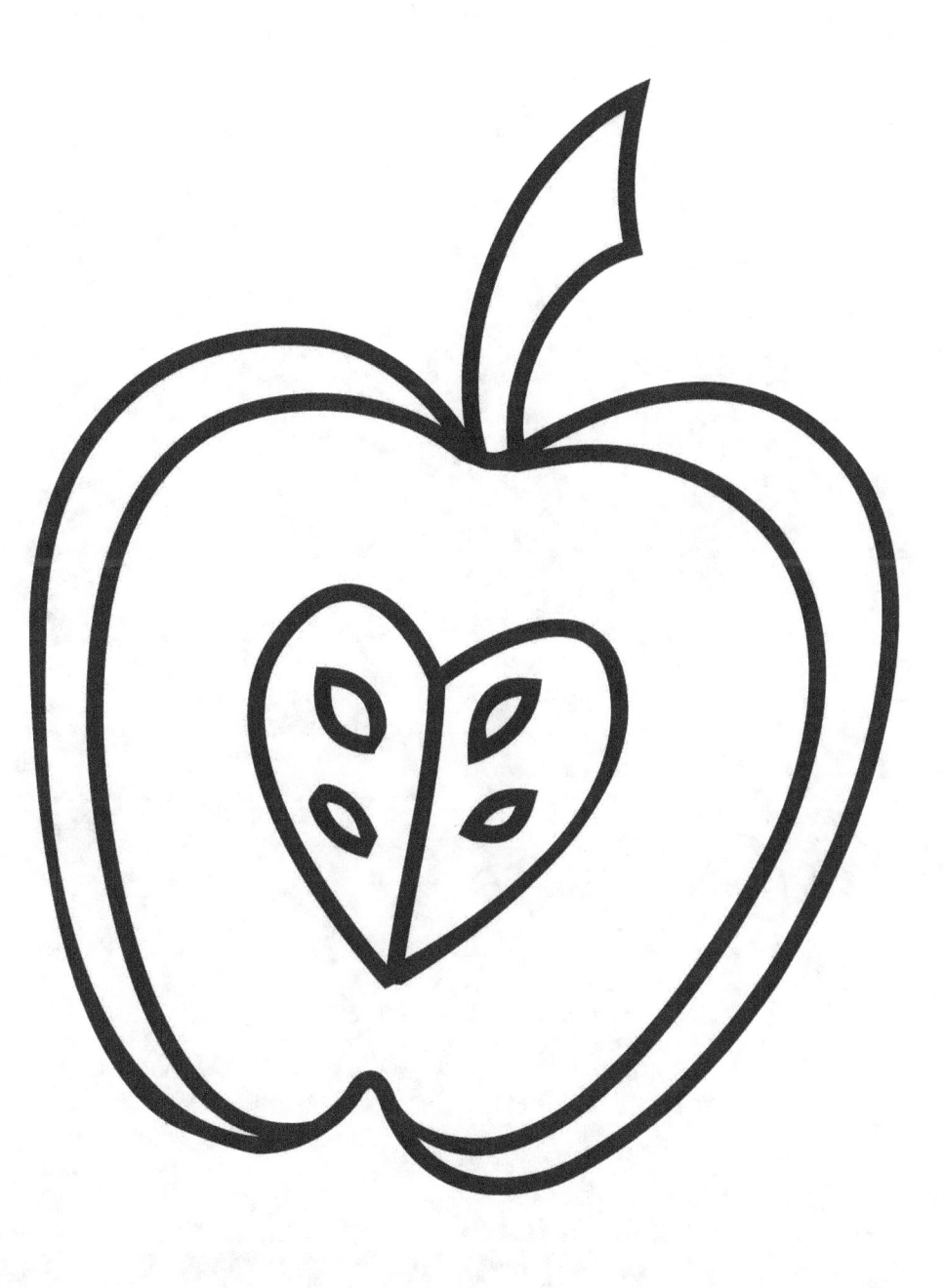

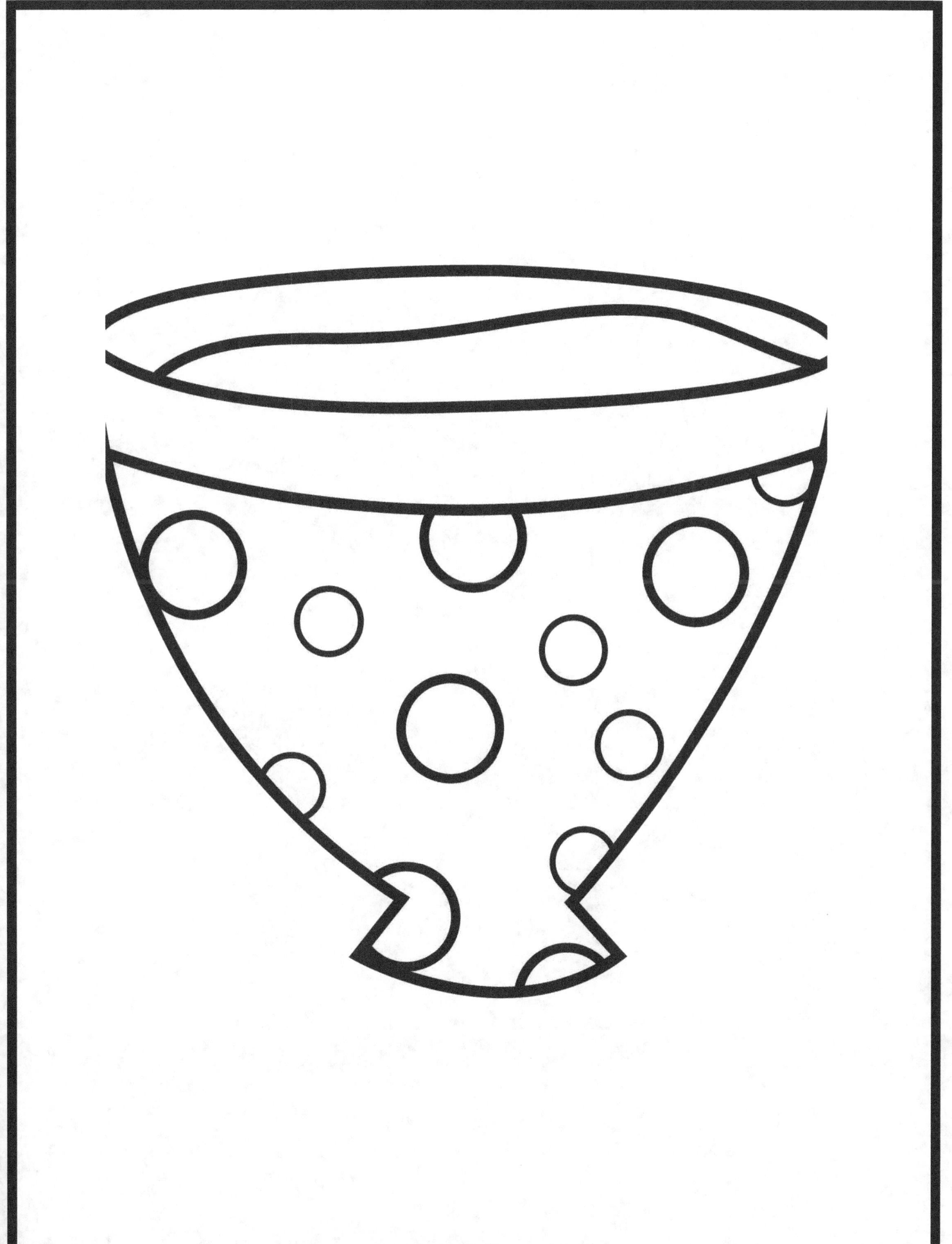

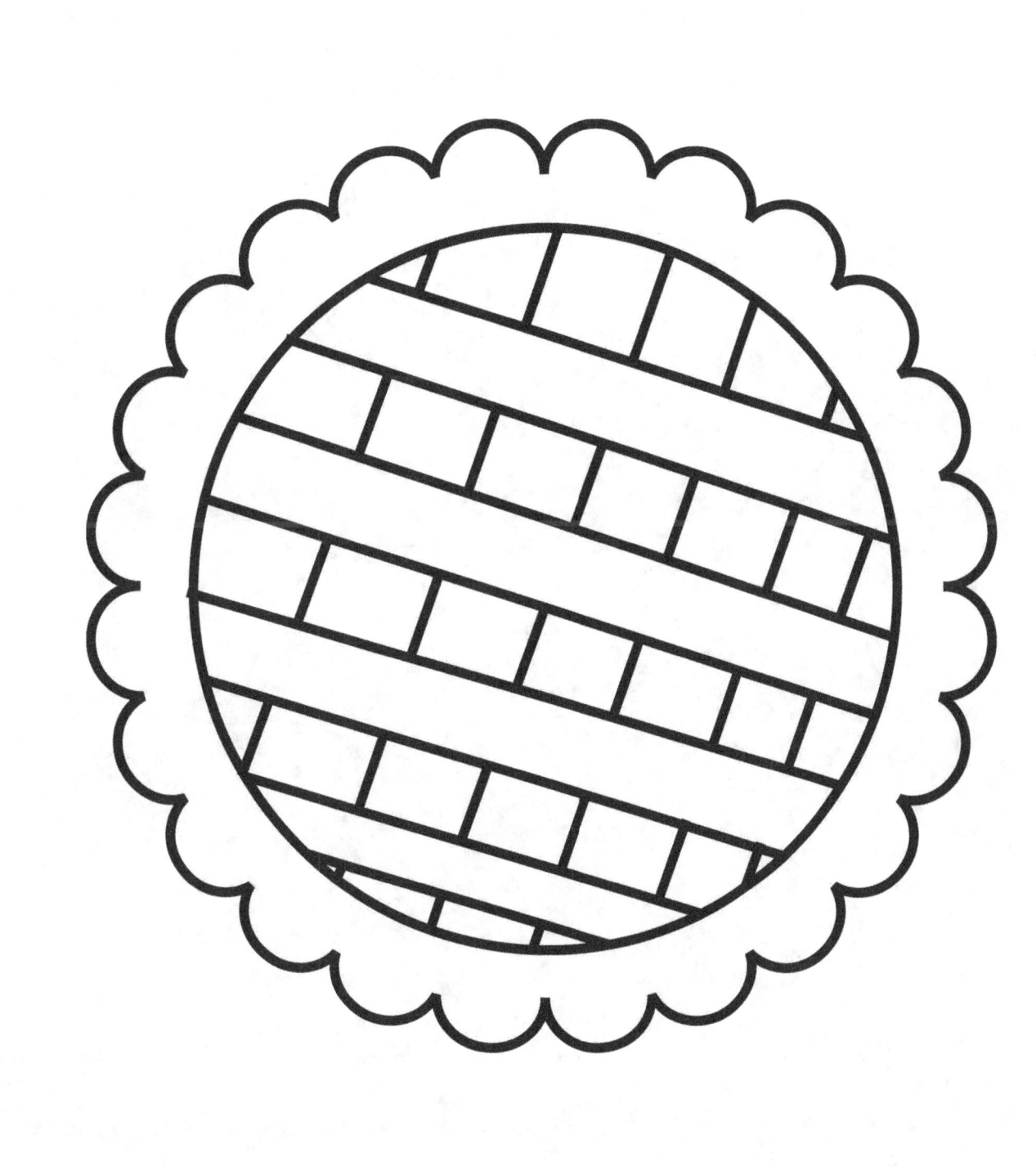

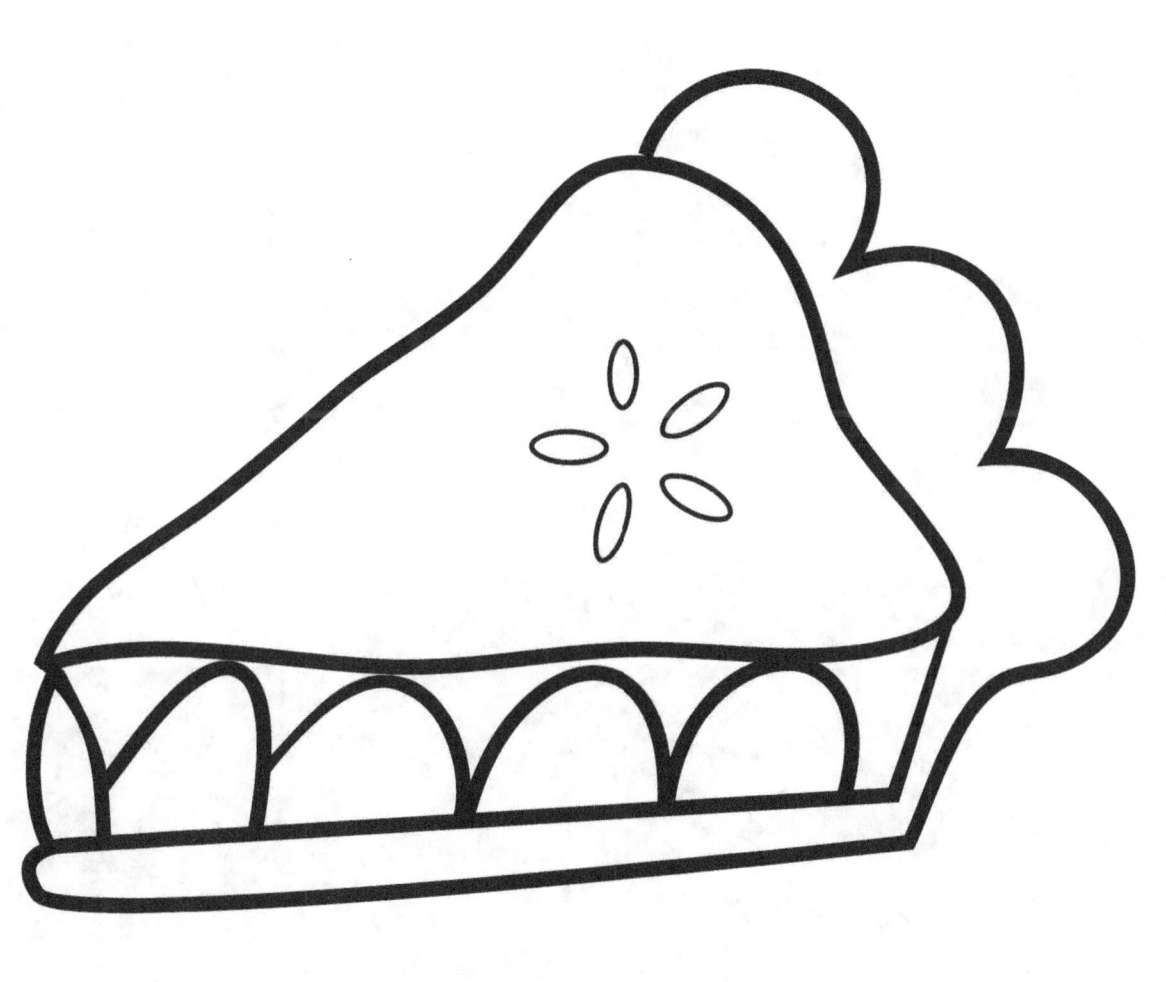

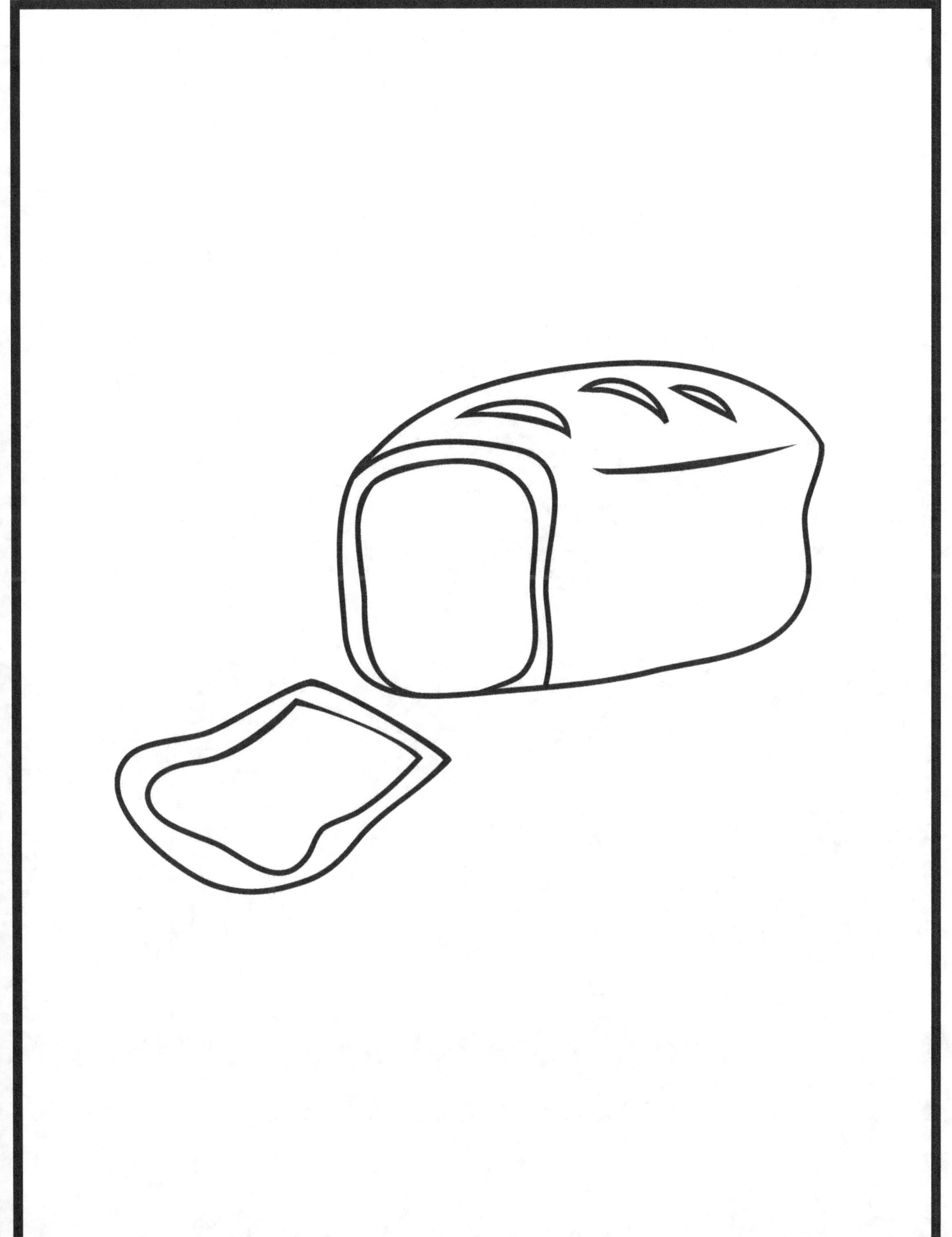

TREAT

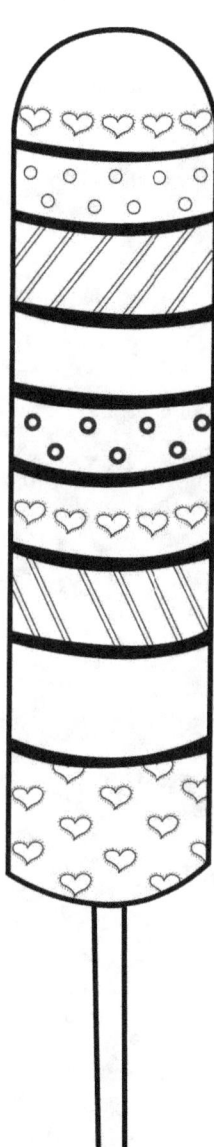

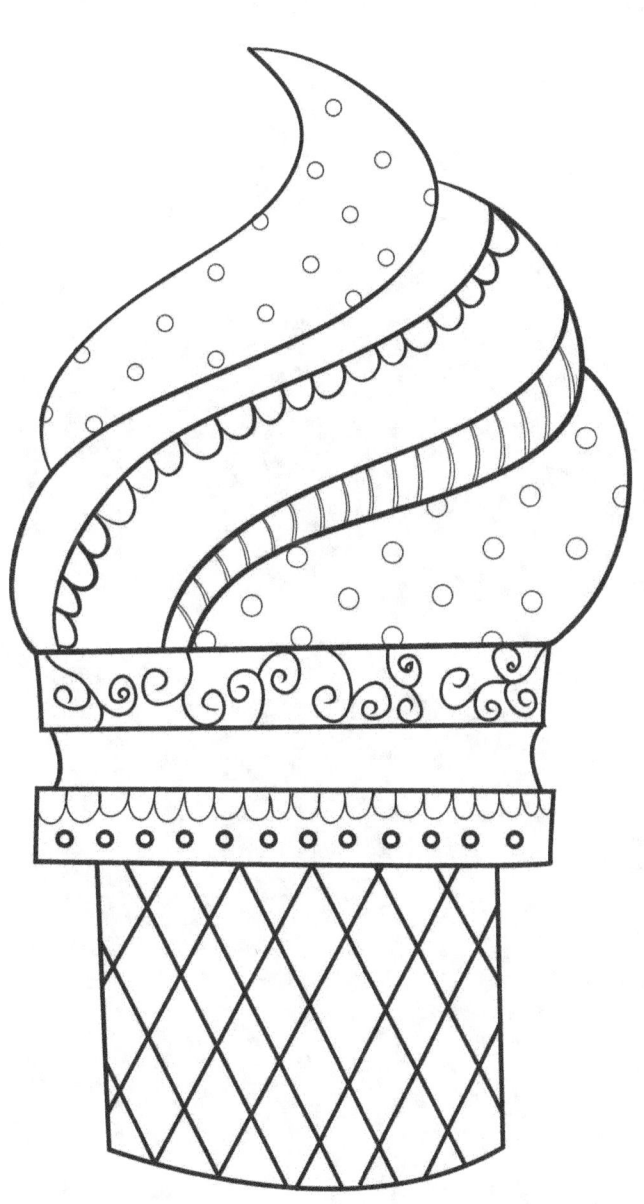

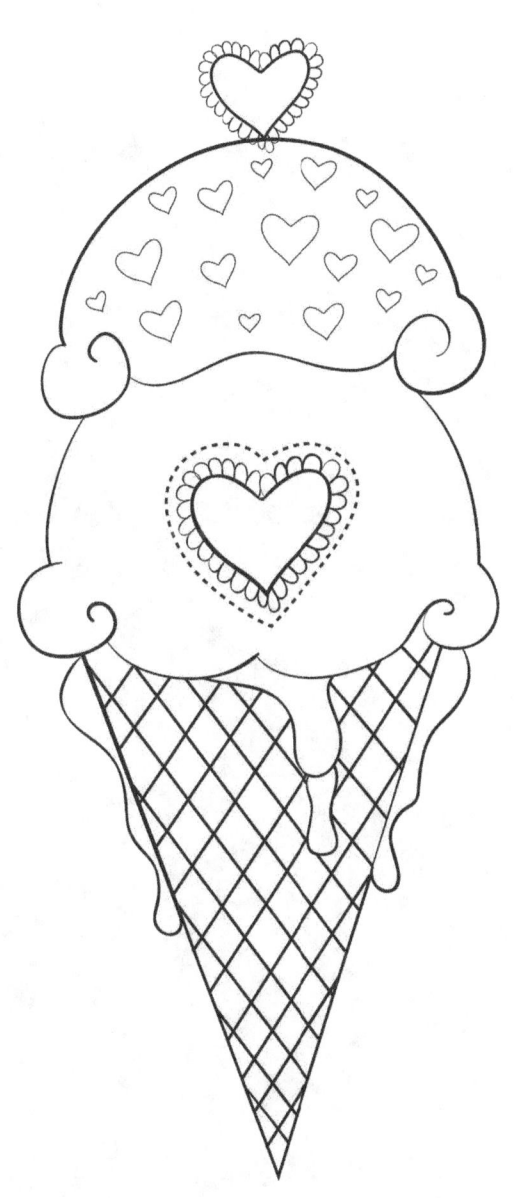

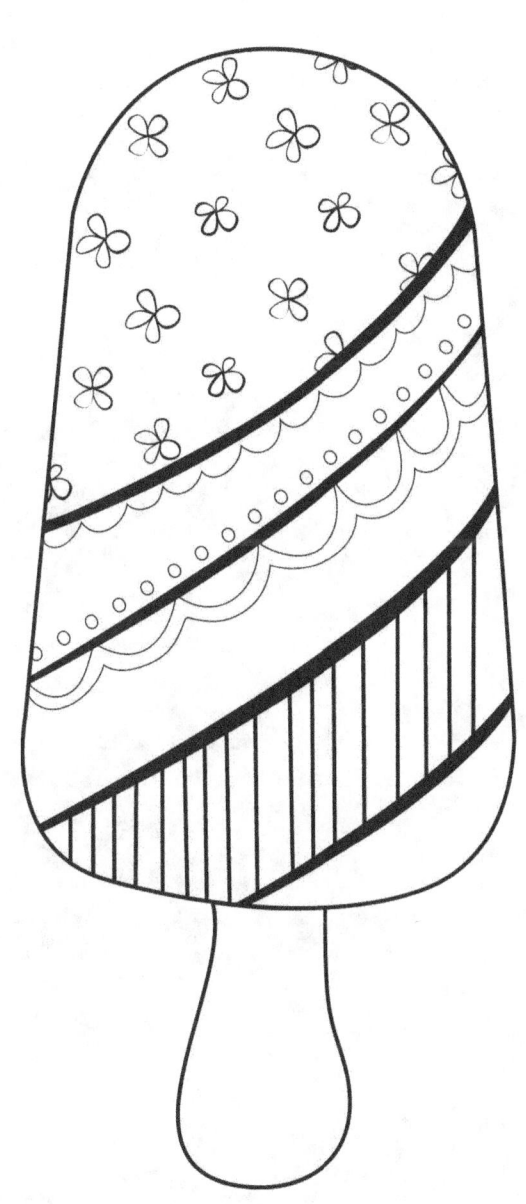

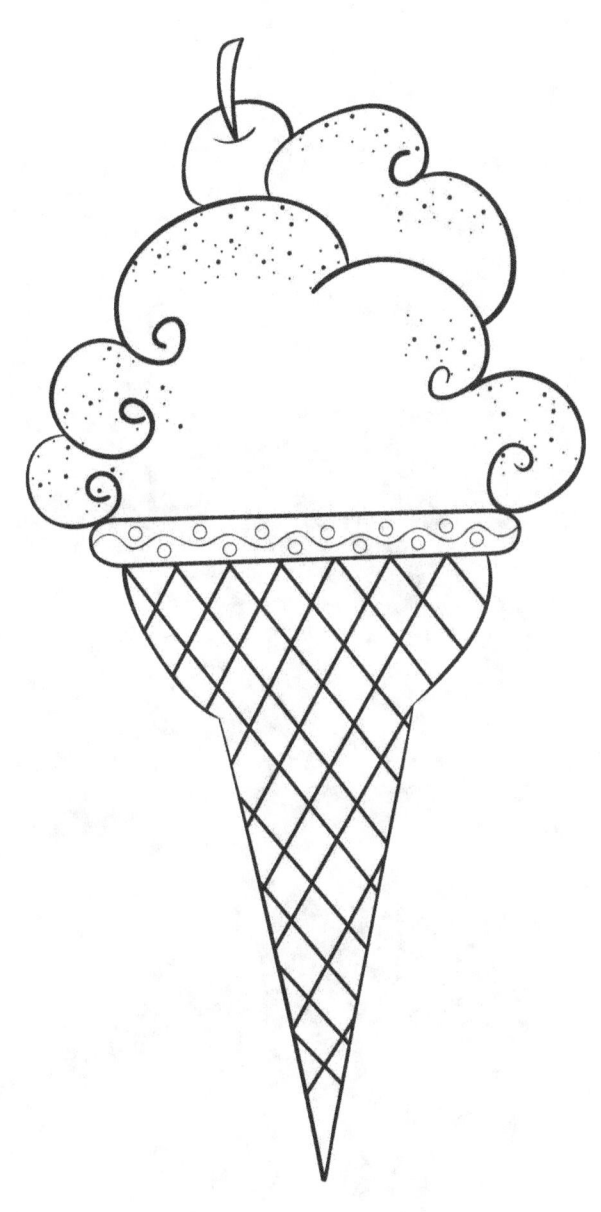

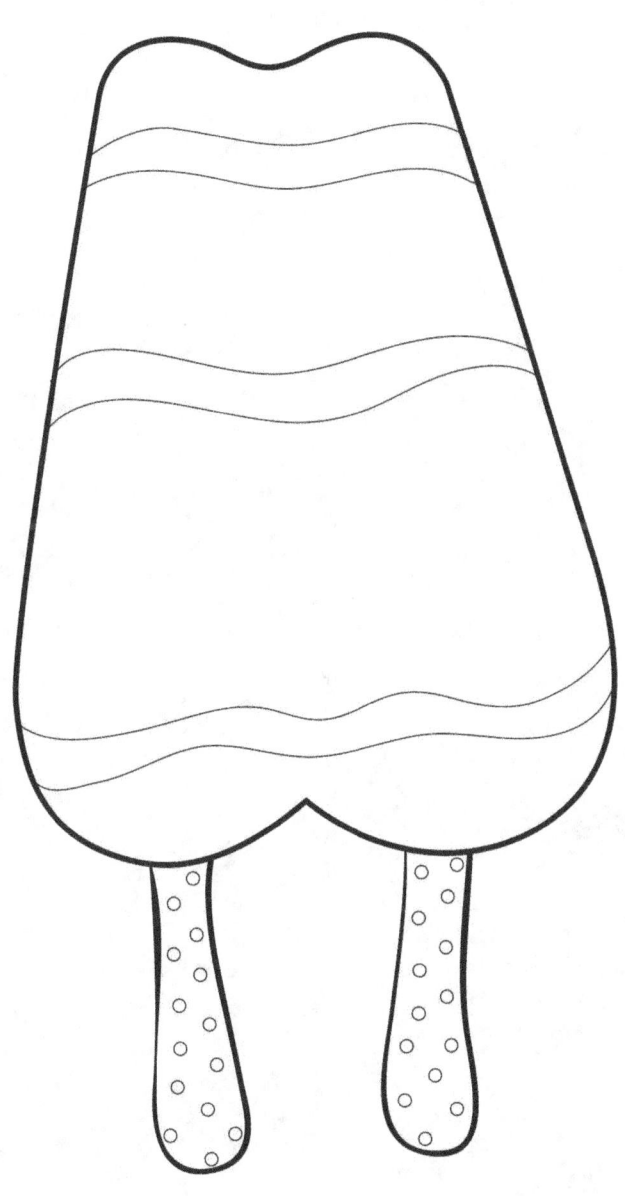

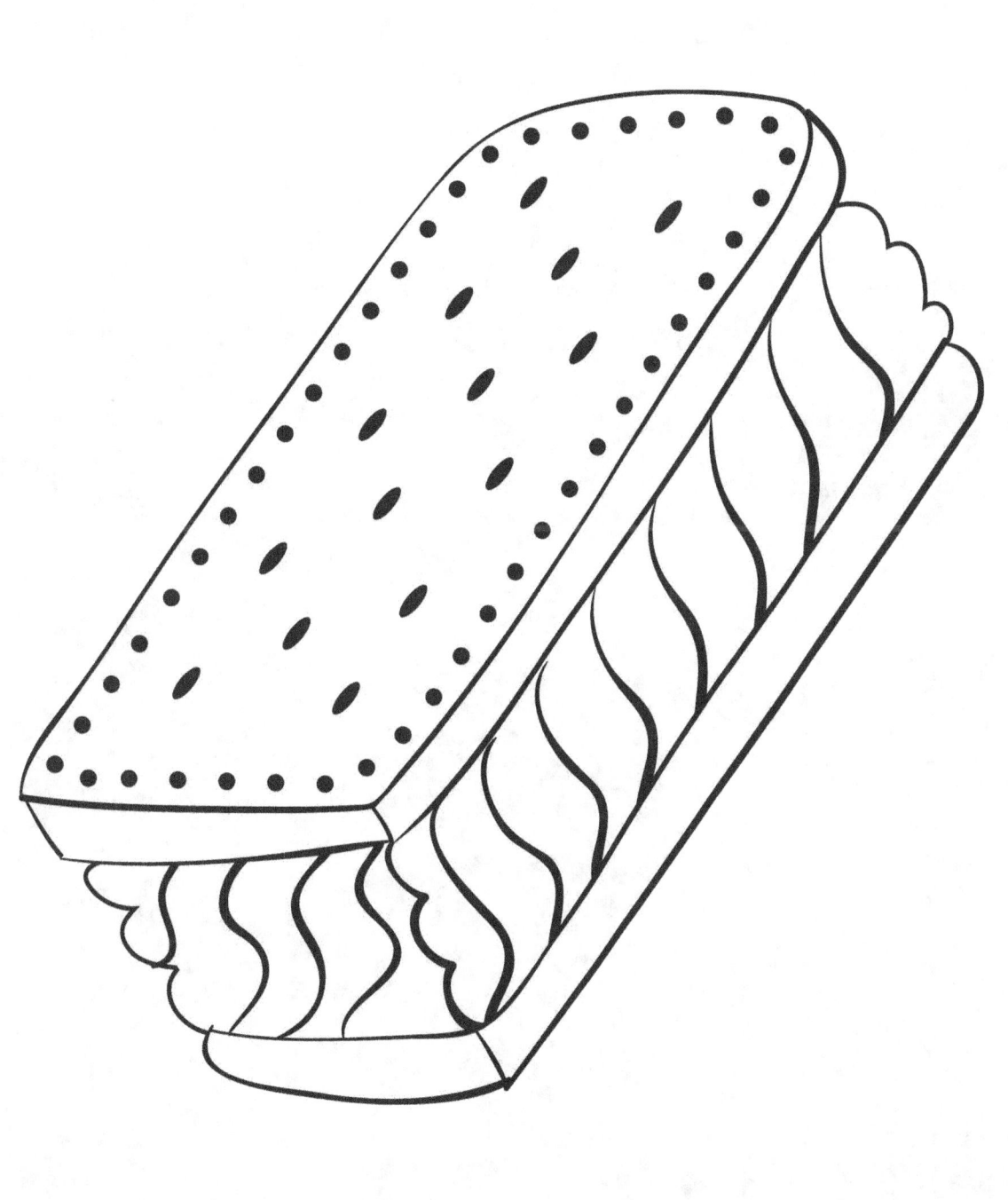

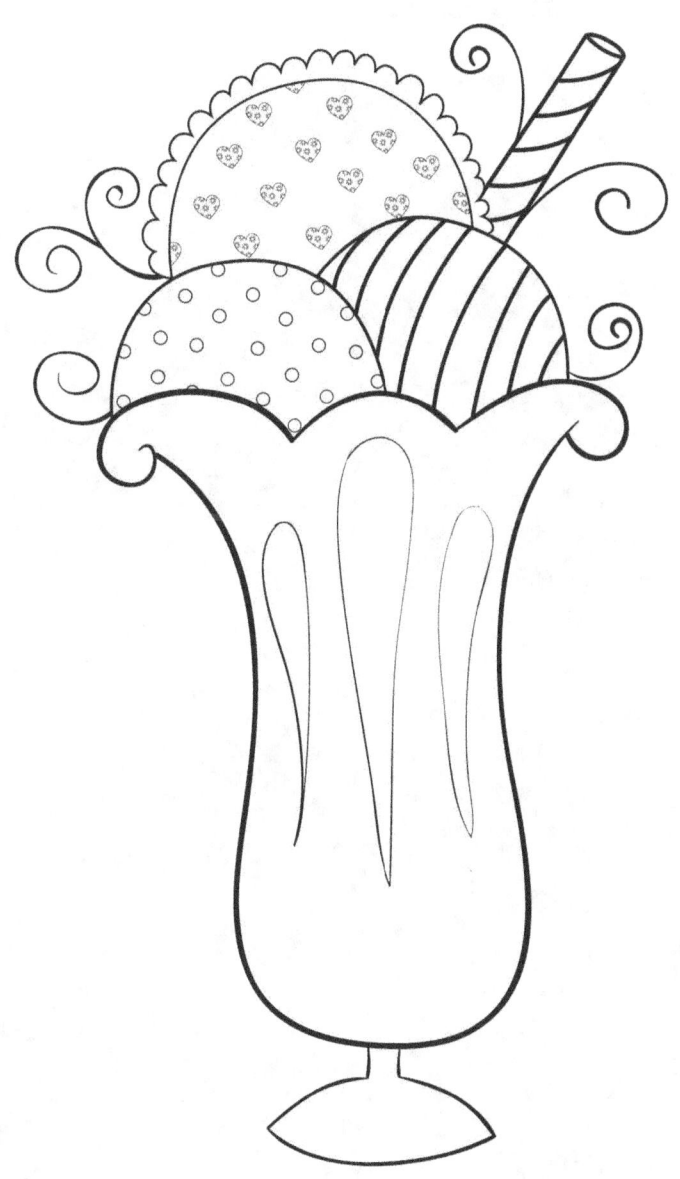

FLOWER

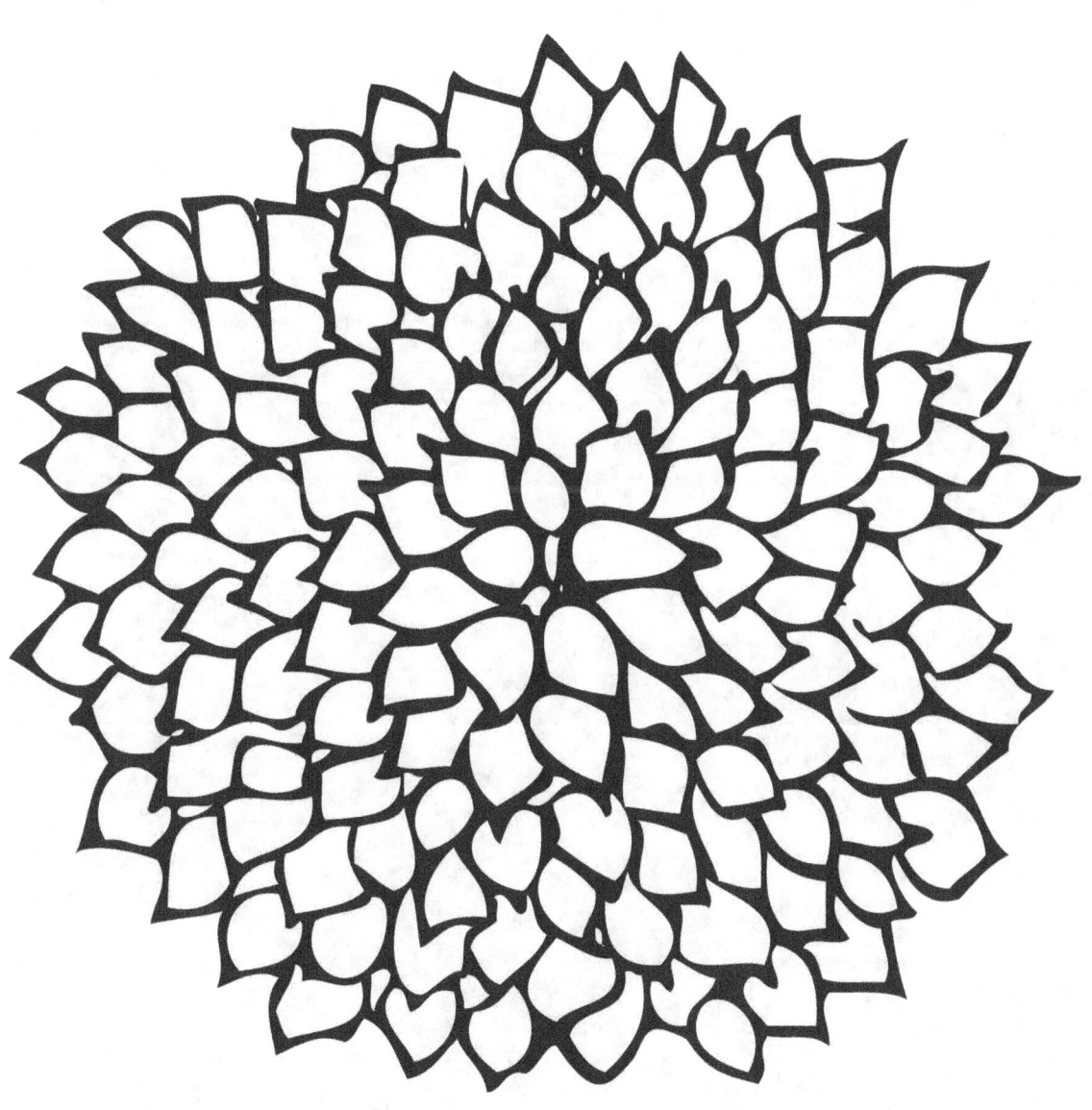

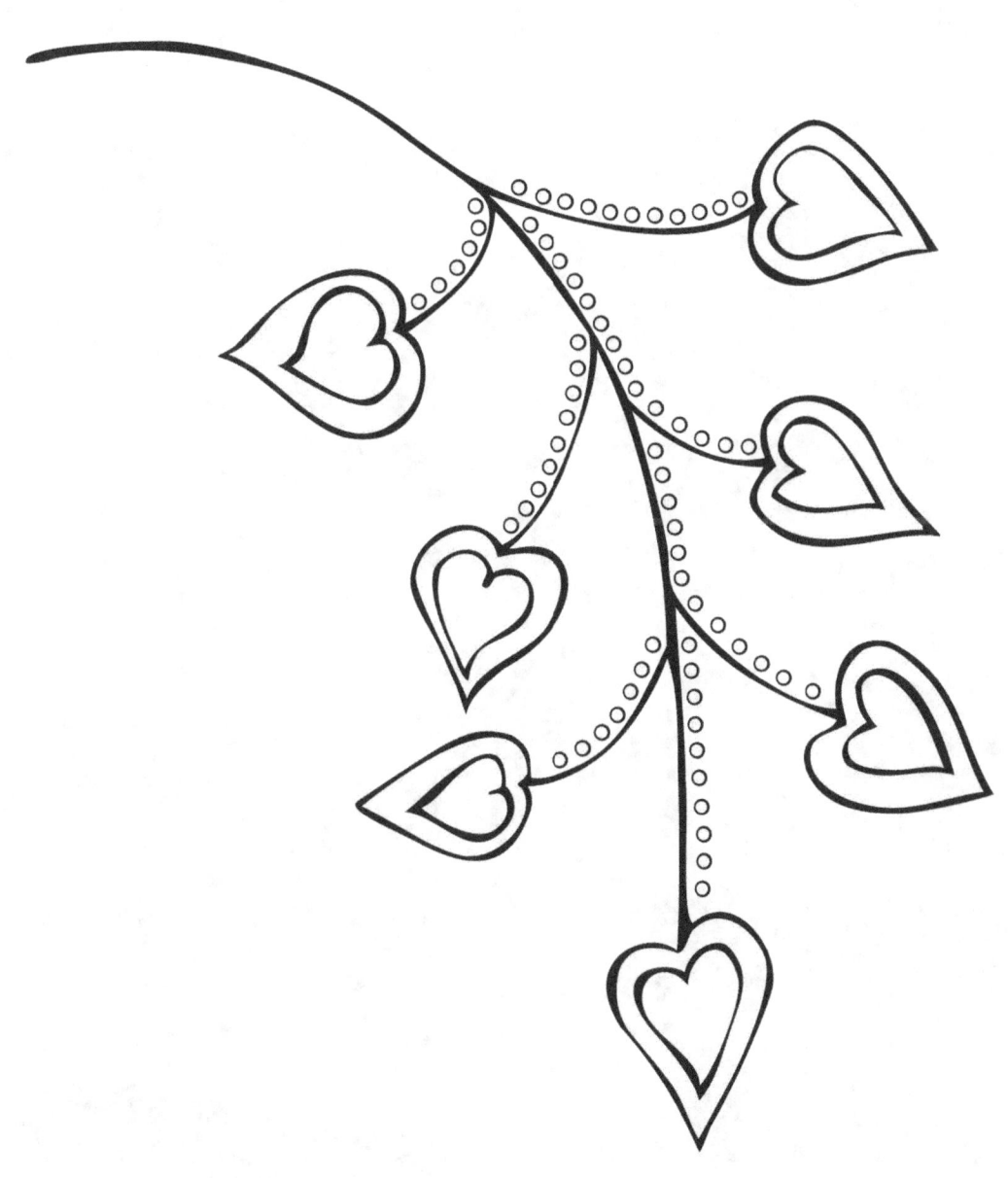

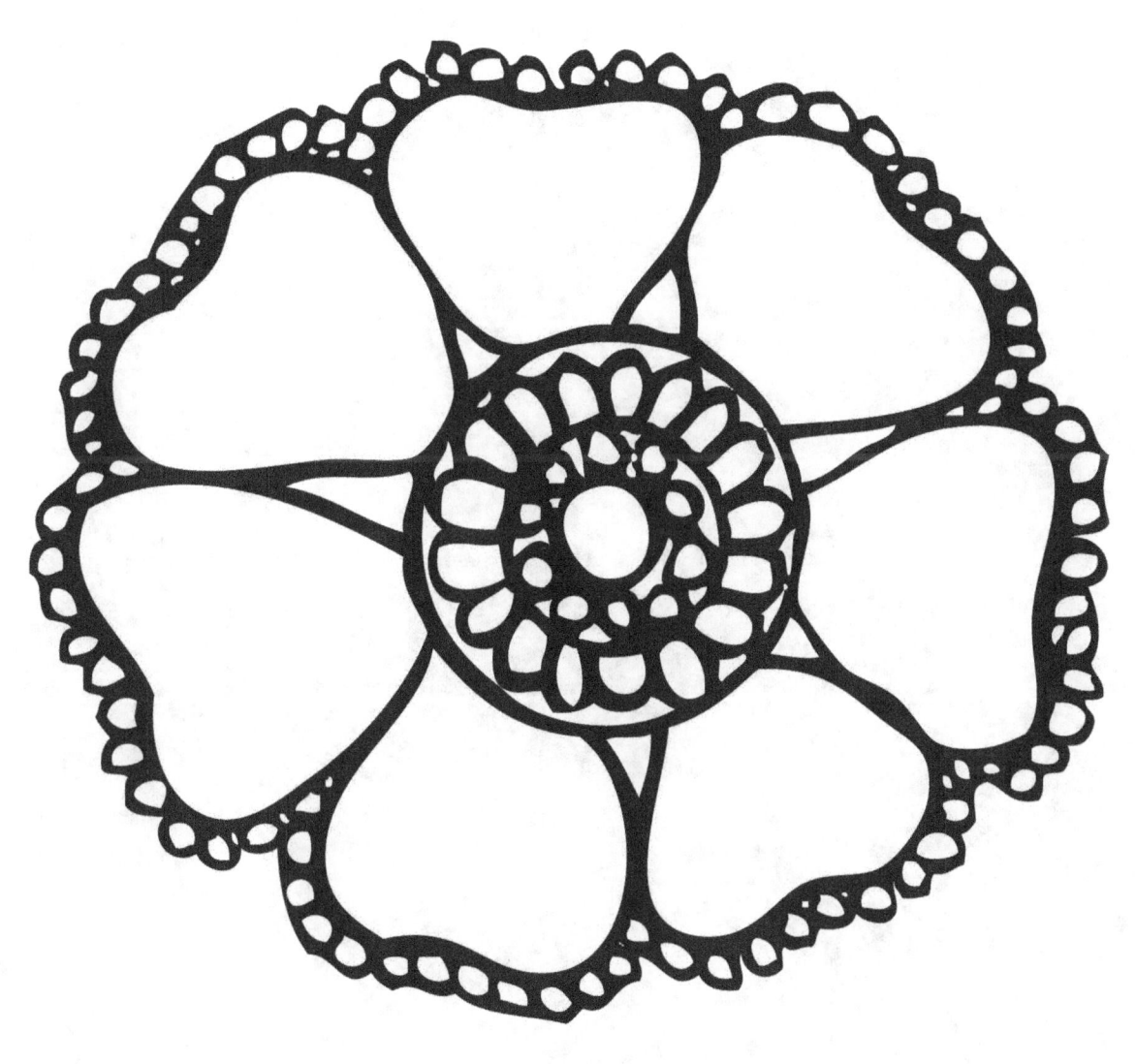

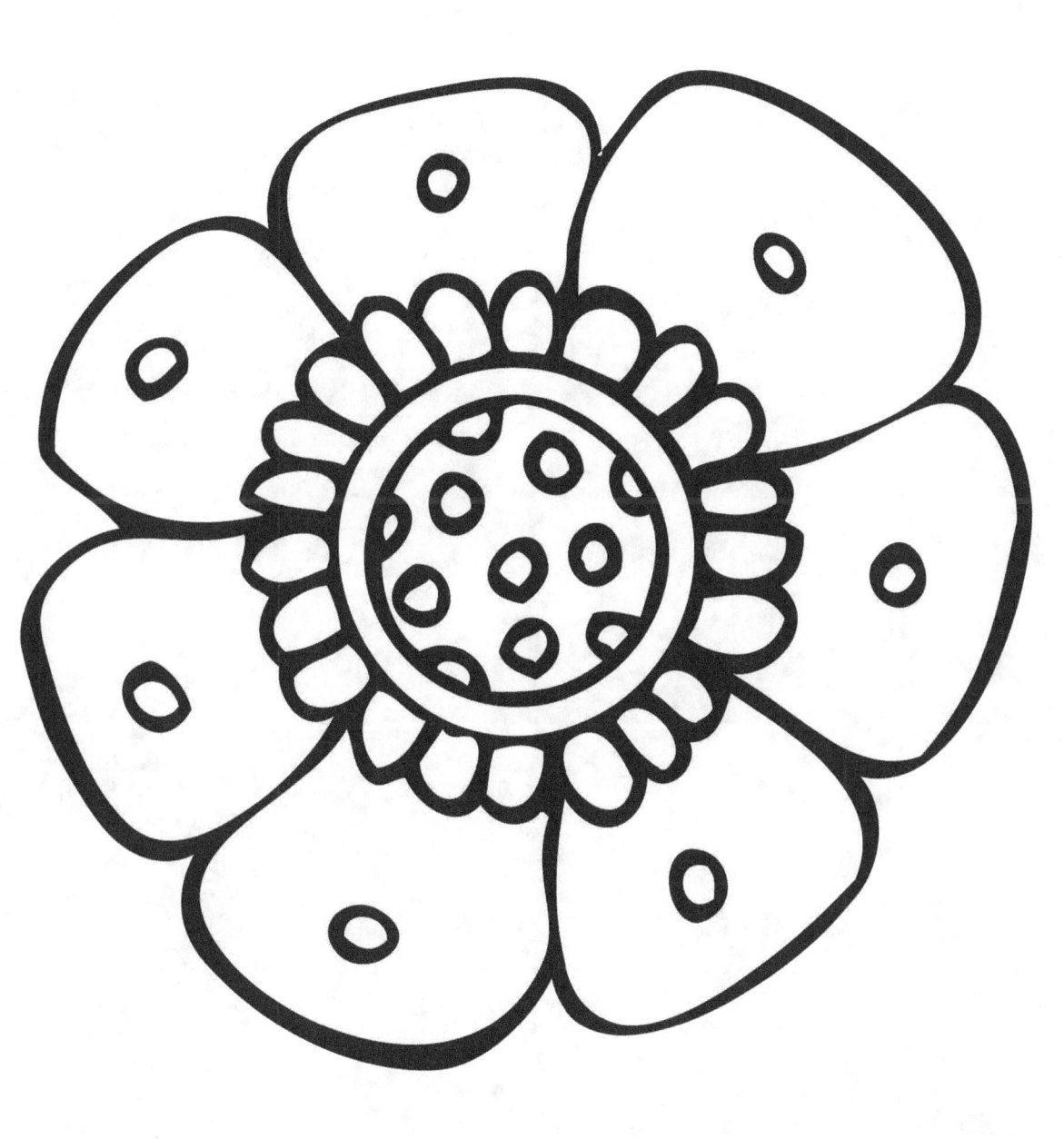

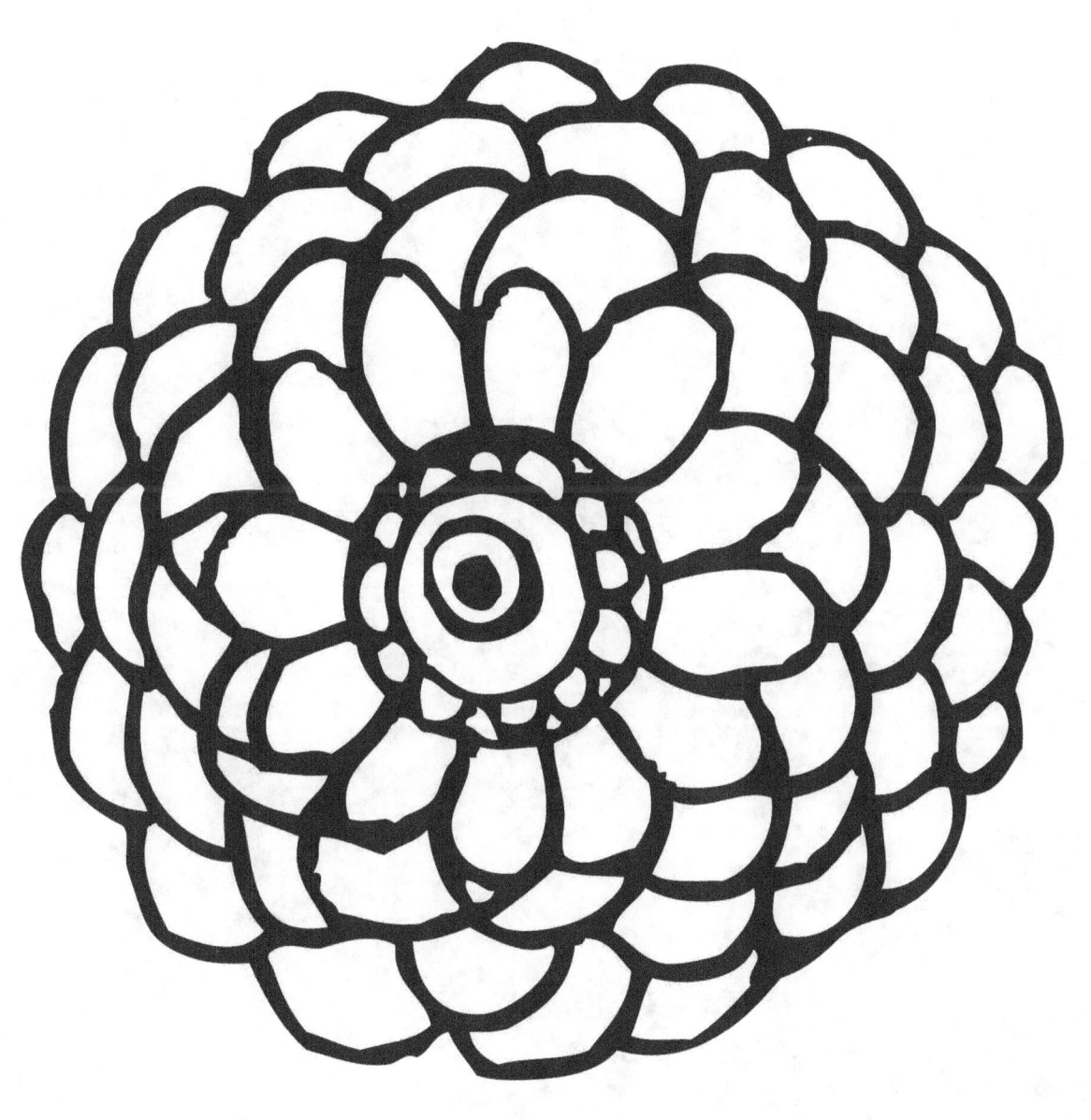

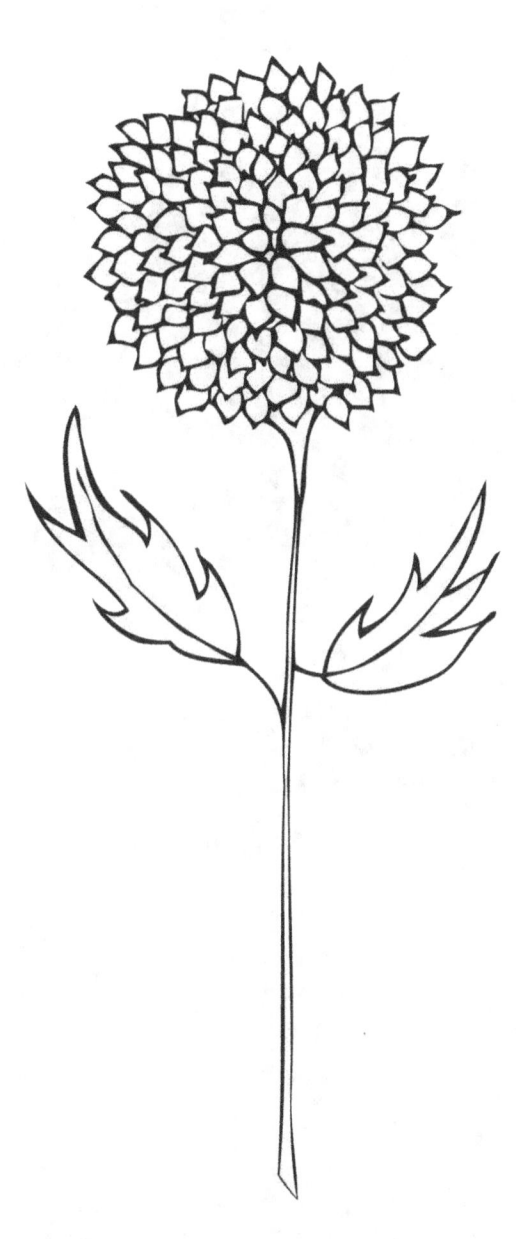

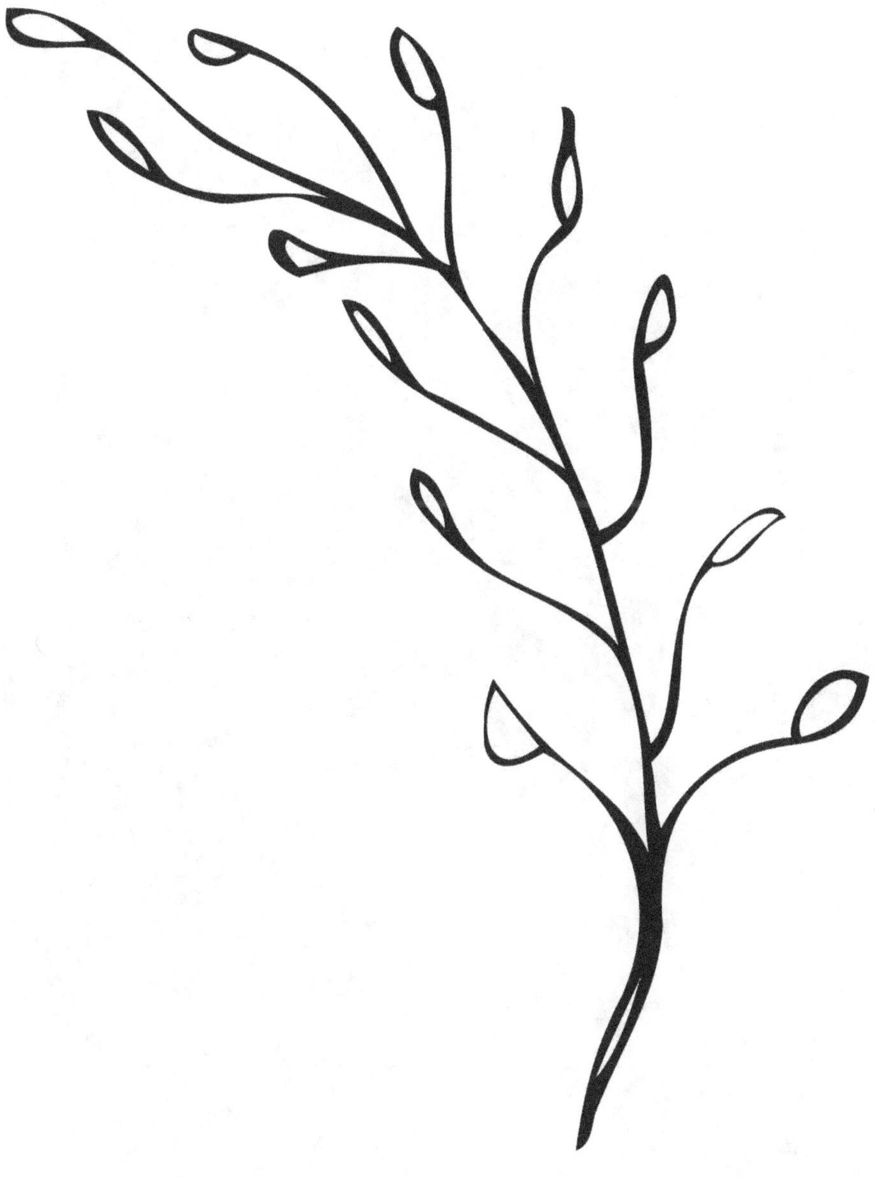

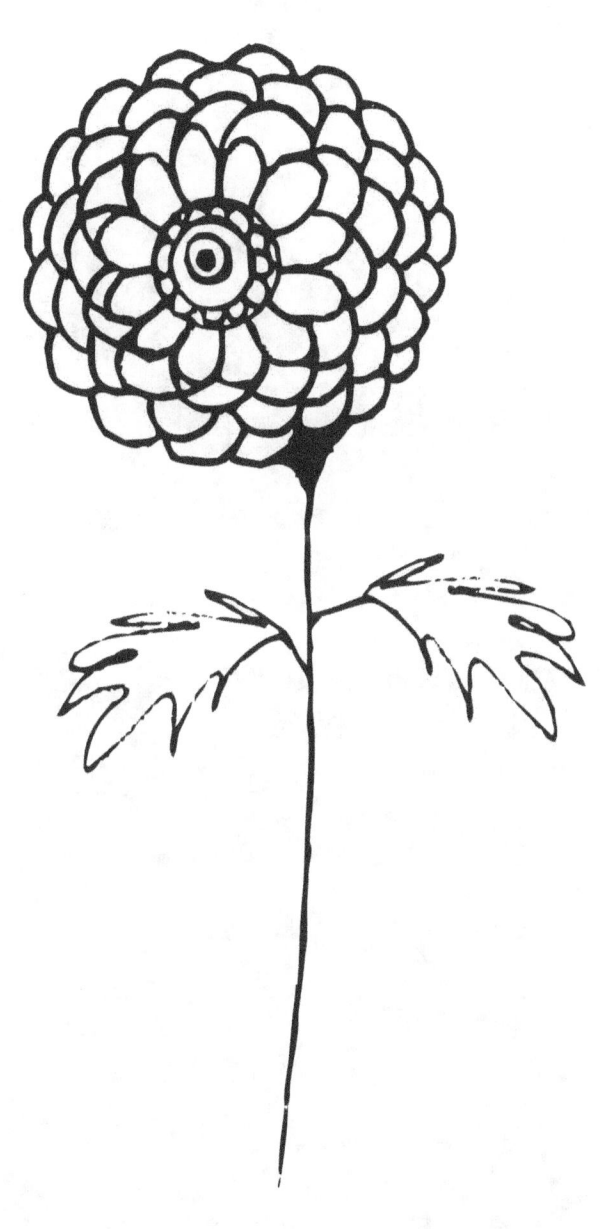

SPACE

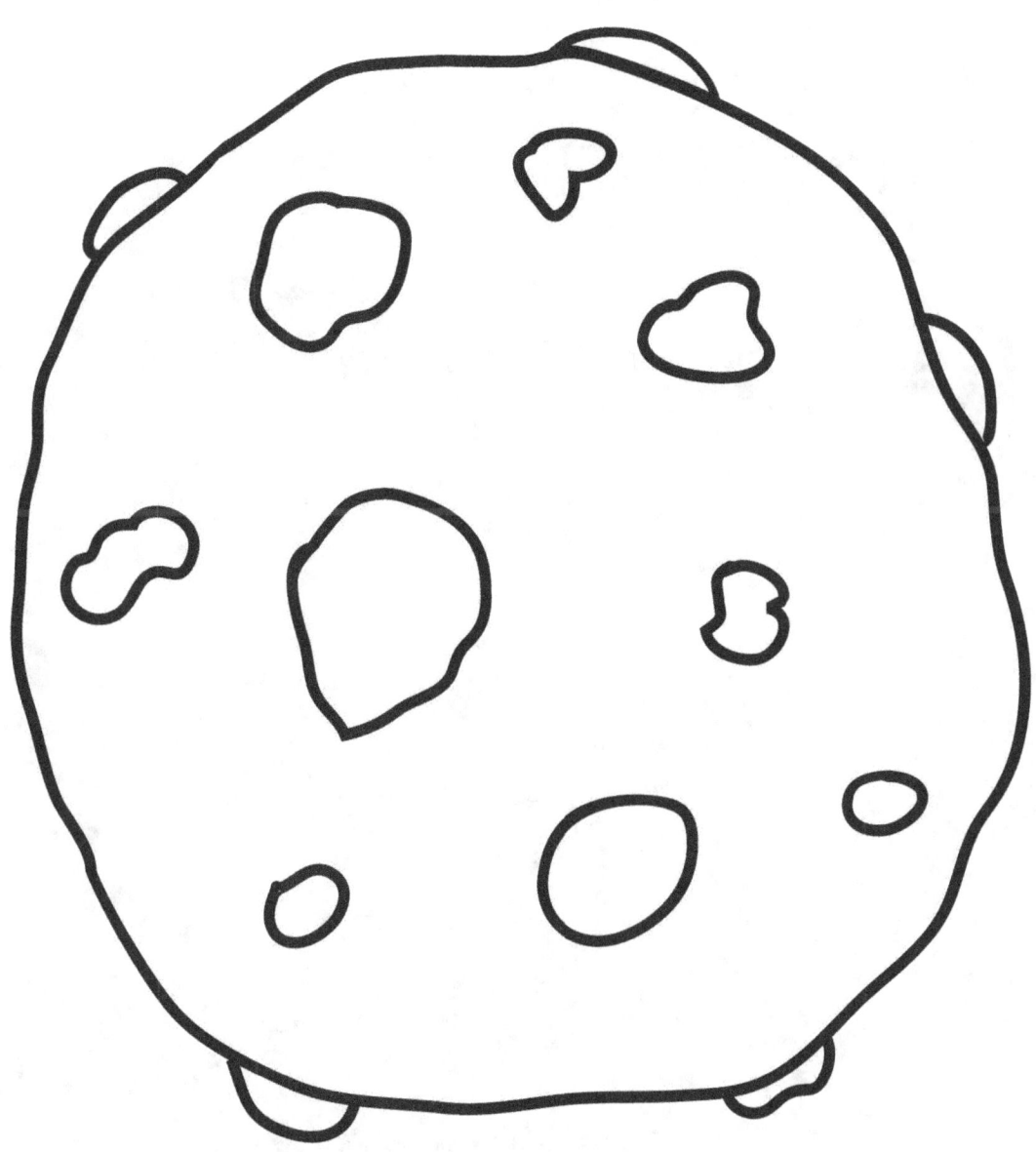

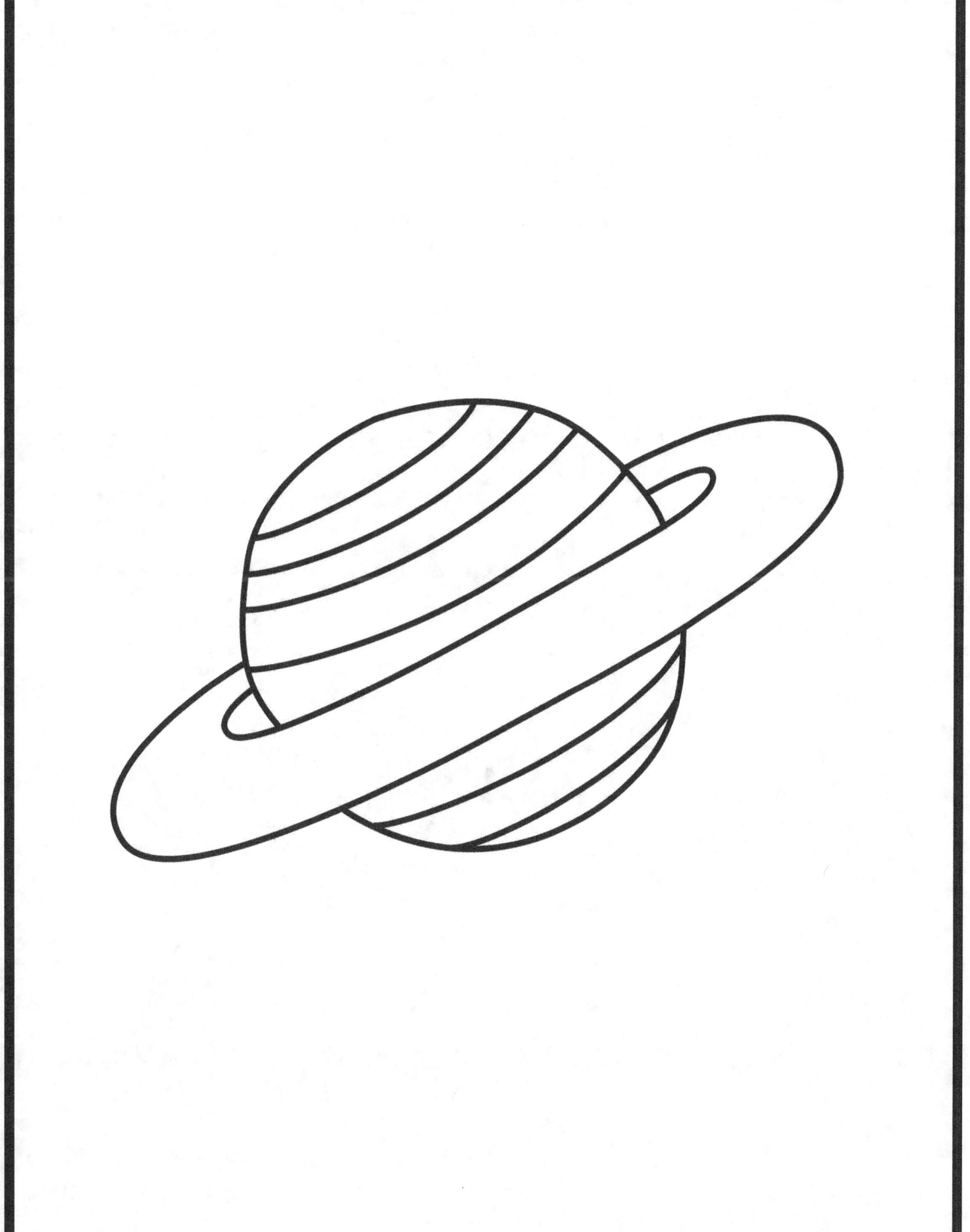

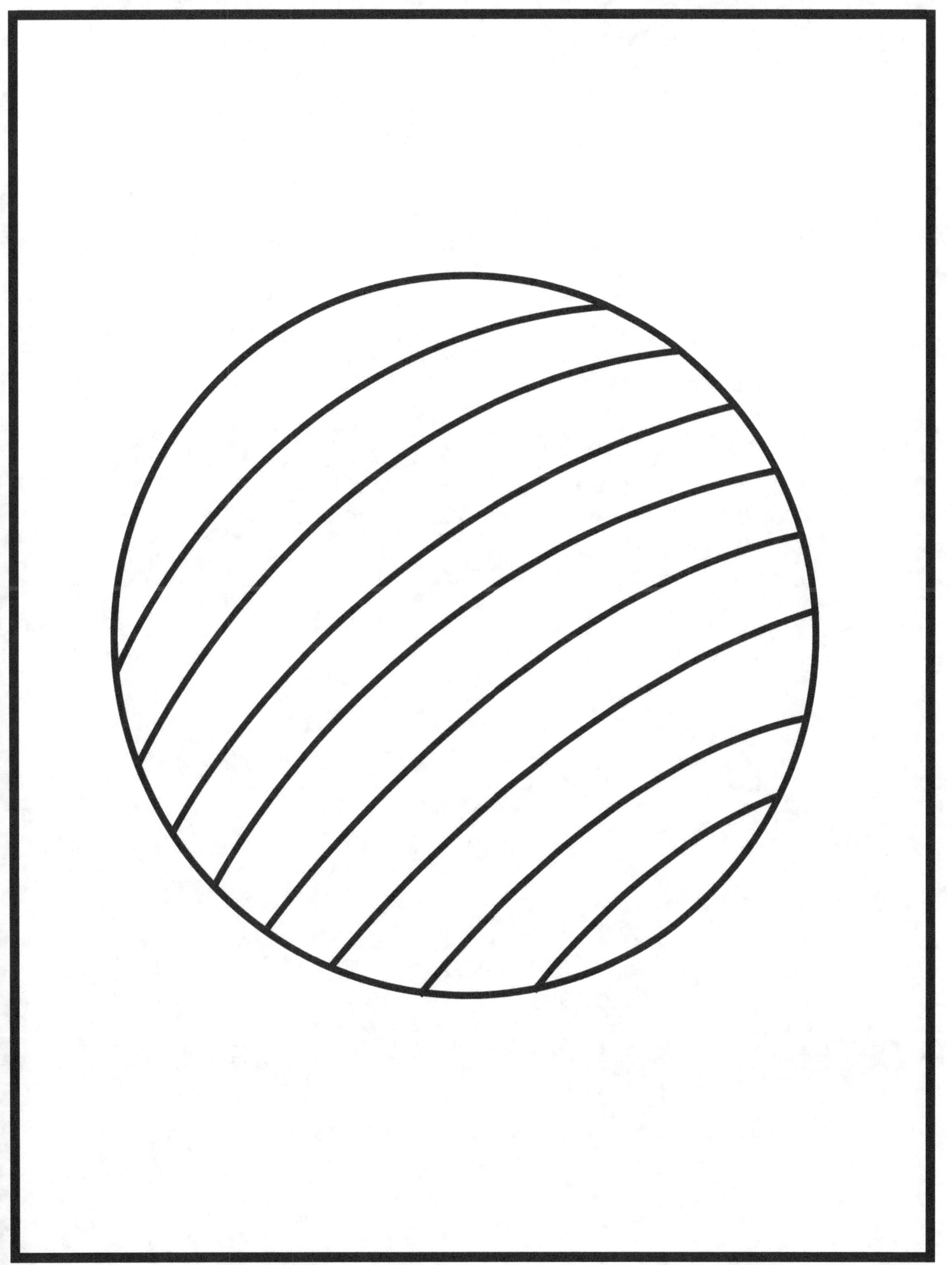

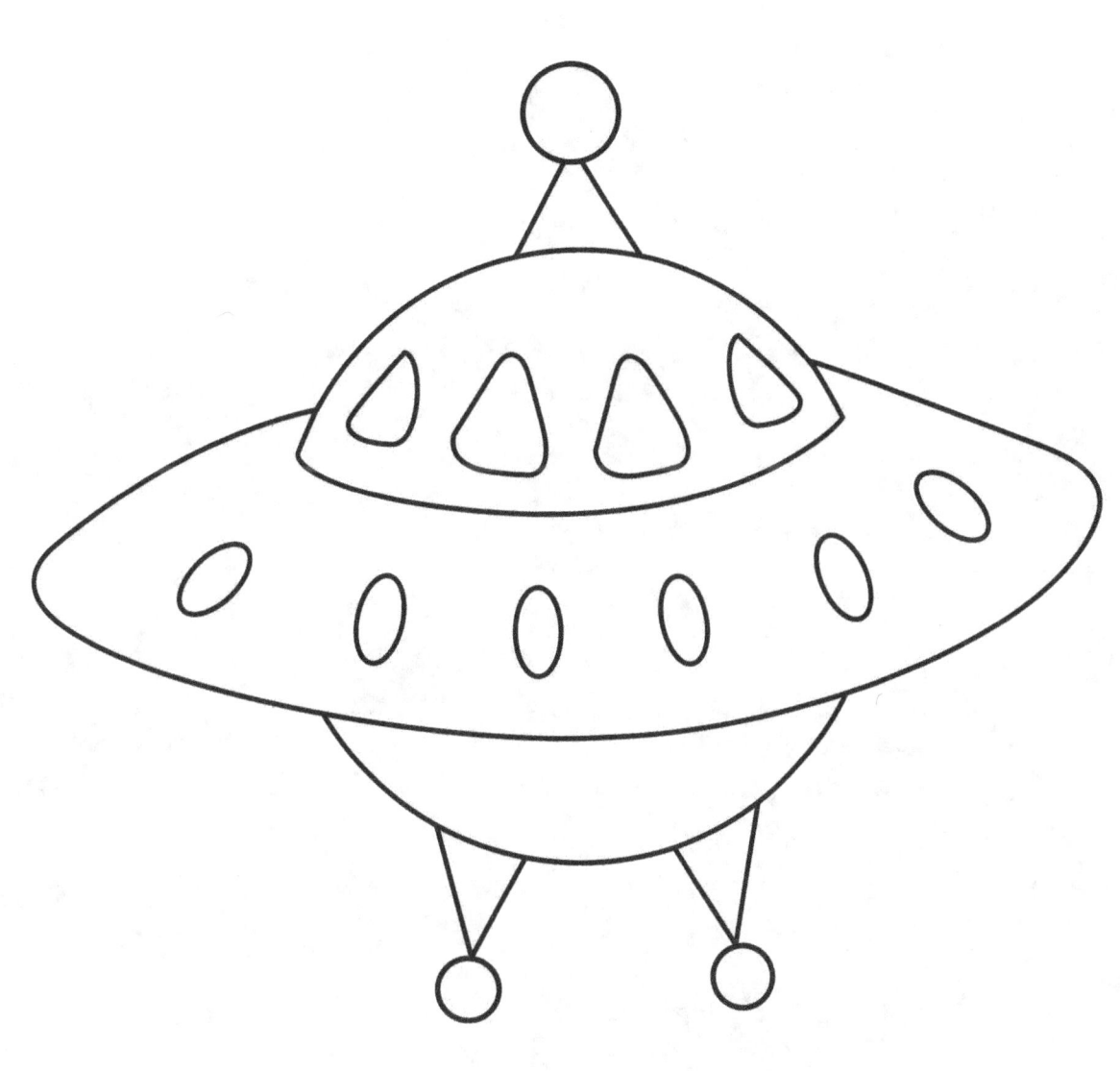

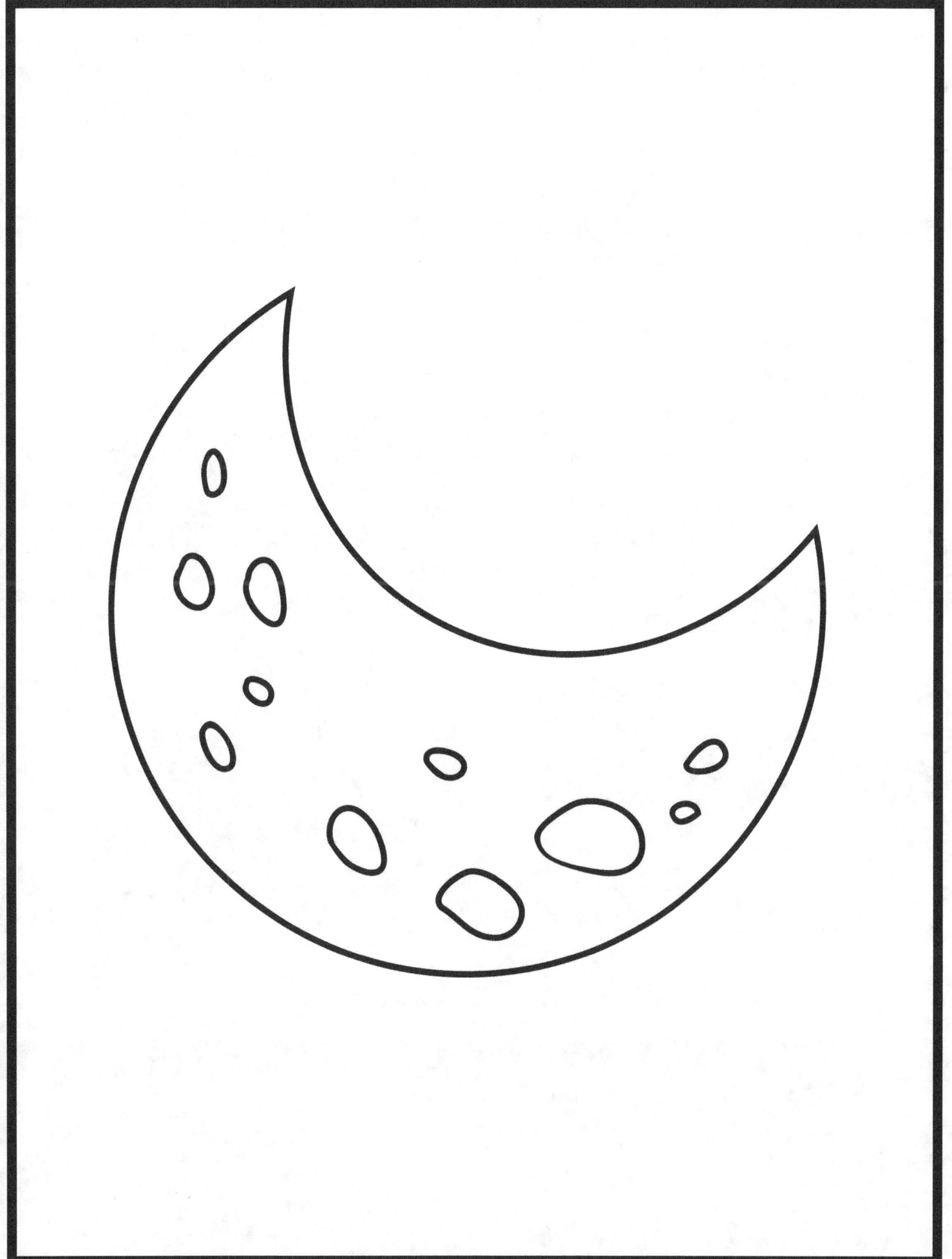

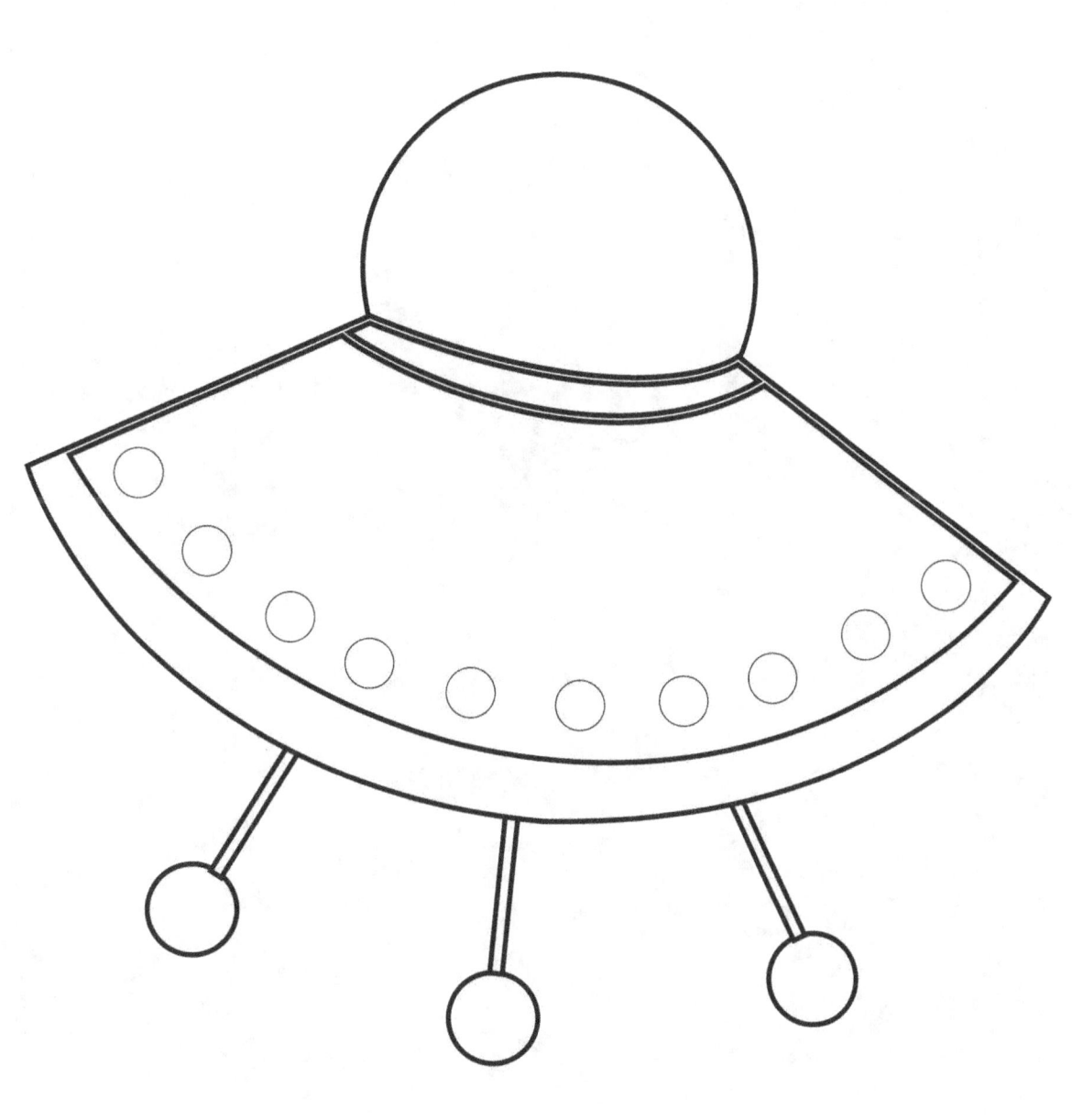

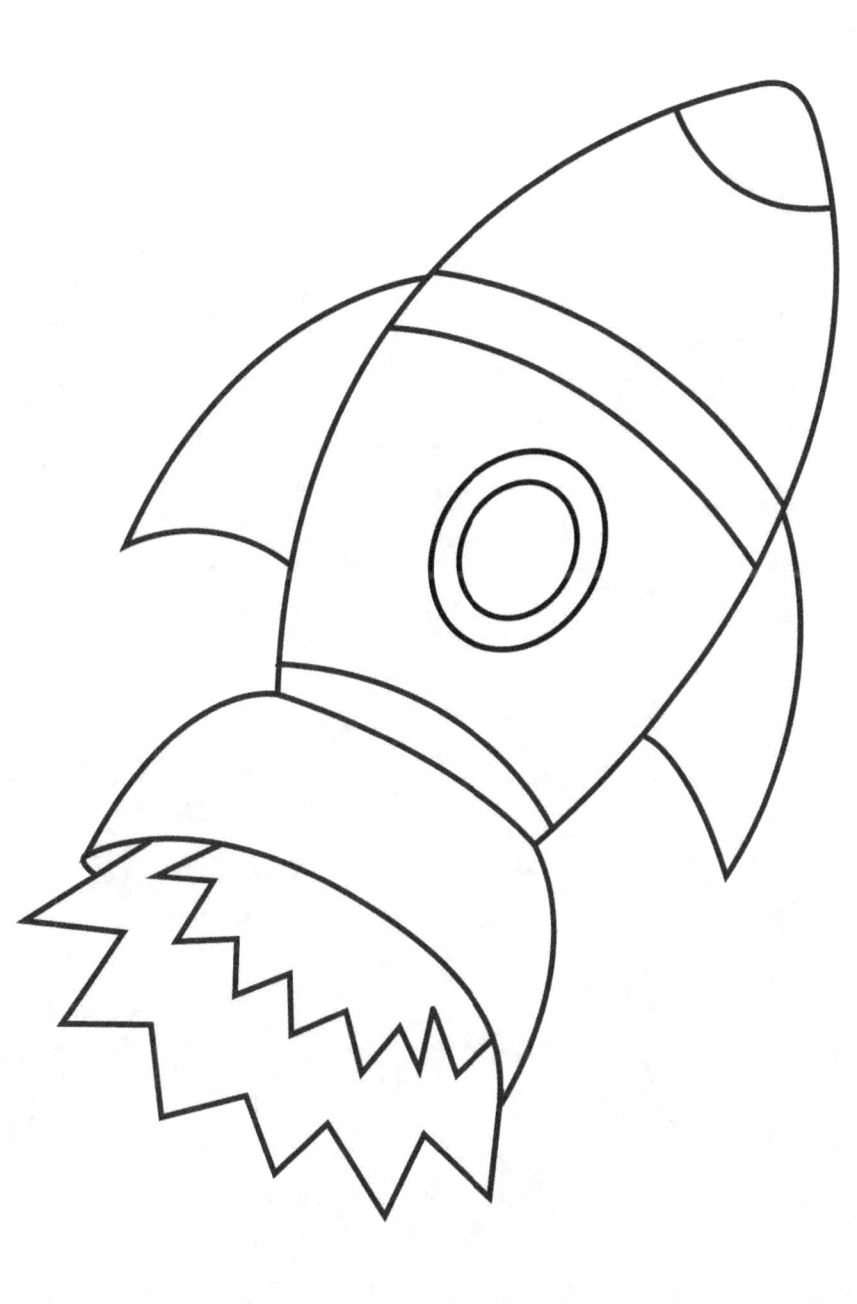

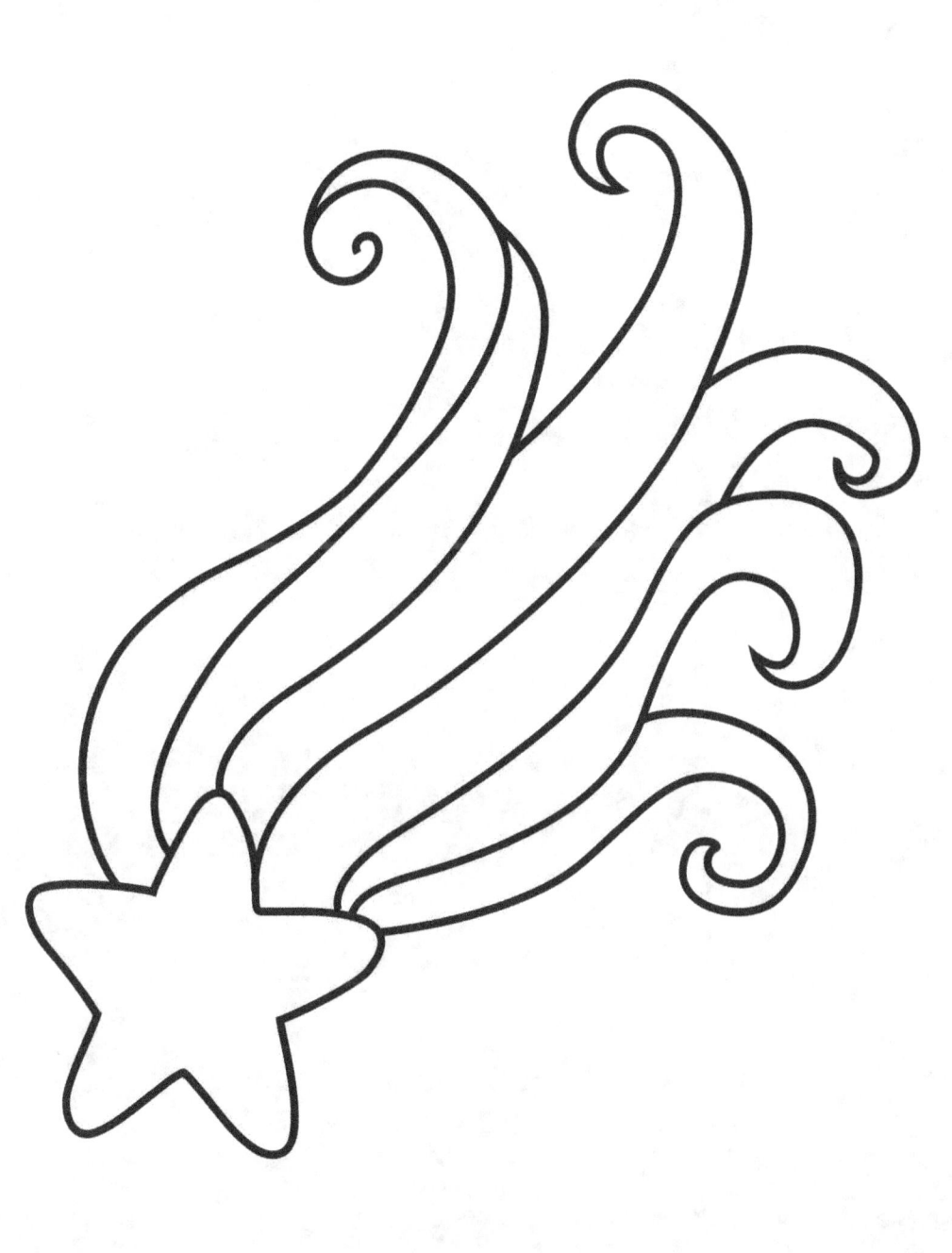

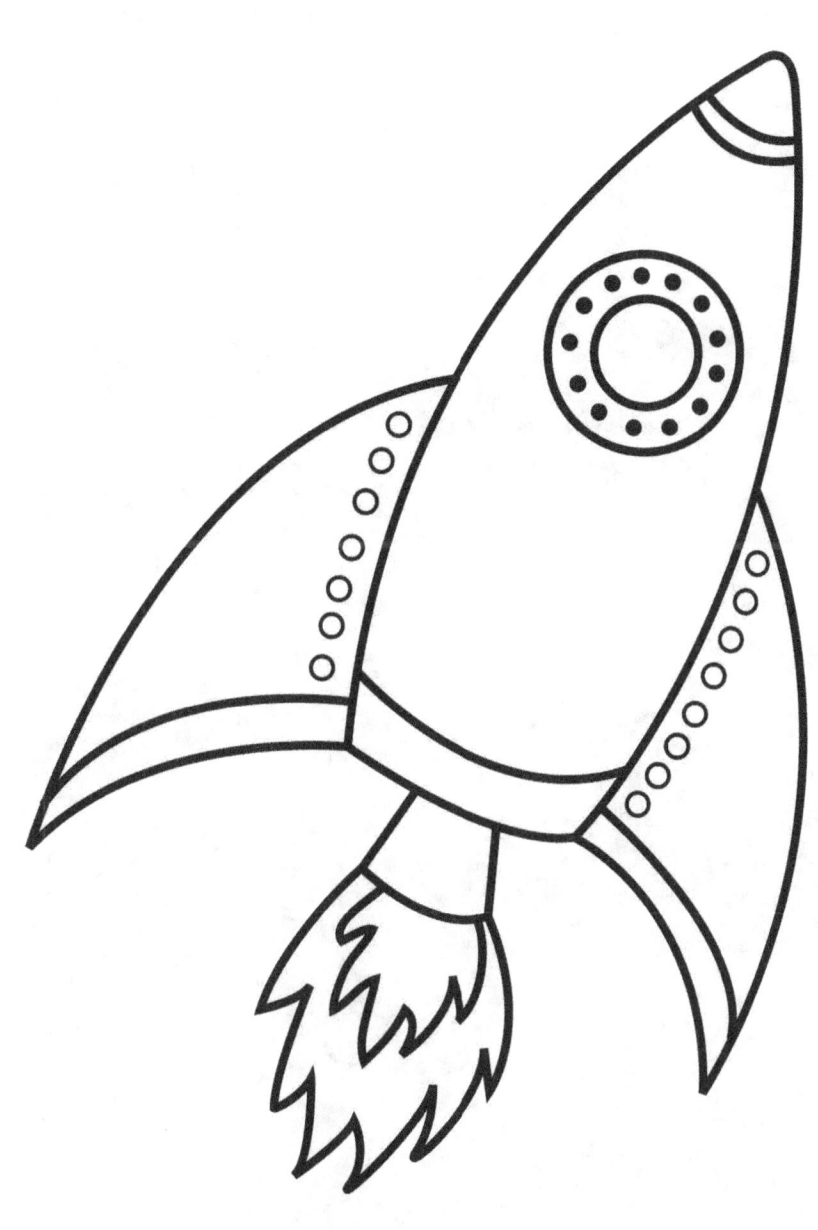

www.ingramcontent.com/pod-product-compliance
Lightning Source LLC
Chambersburg PA
CBHW081517220526
45467CB00010B/2951